Soft Eyes, Strong Spine

A Guide to Life and Kids from a Divorced Dad

Eric Brockman

Soft Eyes Strong Spine Press
An imprint of Soft Eyes Strong Spine, LLC
Gastonia, North Carolina
softeyesstrongspine.com

ISBN: 979-8-9945048-1-9 (Hardcover)
ISBN: 979-8-9945048-2-6 (Paperback)
ISBN: 979-8-9945048-3-3 (eBook)

First Edition
Printed in the United States of America

Cover design by Allison Janicki
Interior design by Allison Janicki
Line editing by Erica Ellis, Ink Deep Editing
Proofreading by Maria VerMulm, The Editor's Margin

DEDICATION

For my four children:
Everything I became,
I became because I was your dad.
And everything good in me was shaped by loving you.
—Pops

TABLE OF CONTENTS

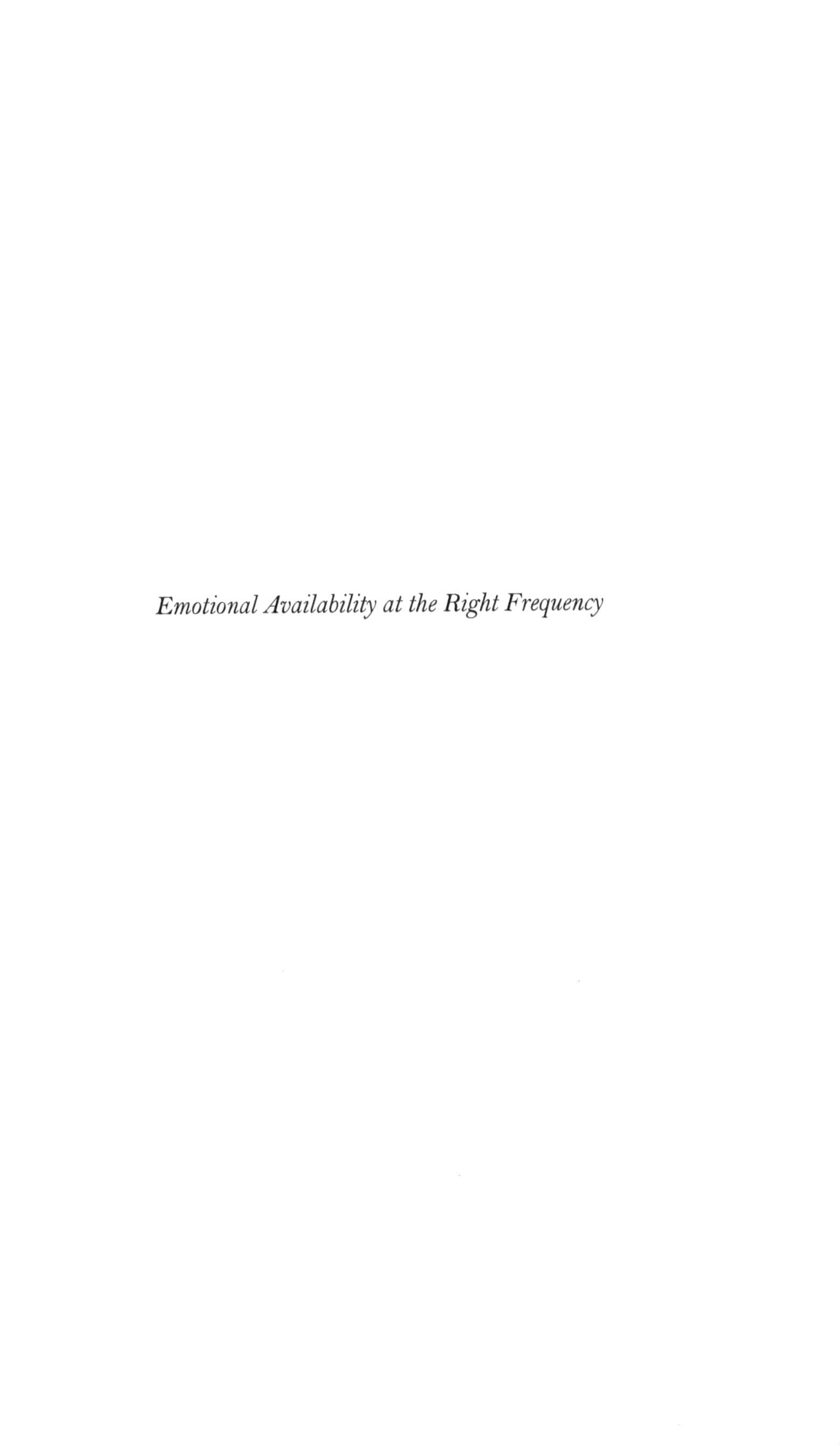

Emotional Availability at the Right Frequency

INTRODUCTION

Most men don't think they're "tightening" up inside. They think they're "handling it." Tightening looks normal from the outside. It's your shoulders living a half-inch higher than they need to. It's your jaw doing its own lockdown. It's your brain running scenarios faster than you can keep up with.

This is a book for men—especially fathers in the middle years—who can feel that tension has become their default, and who don't want to pass it on at home.

After divorce, tightening gets promoted. You're not just managing your own life—you're managing drop-offs, calendars, tone, texts, new dynamics, old triggers, and the part of you that still wants to win arguments that aren't even happening anymore.

Sometimes the loudest fight is the one you don't have out loud. It's the one you have in the space between a message and your reply. Thumb hovering. Chest tight. Mind sprinting.

I lived there. For many years, I confused pressure for strength. I confused vigilance for leadership. I thought if I stayed keyed up, I could keep everyone safe. I didn't know I was broadcasting that tension to the people I loved the most—especially my kids.

Then something shifted. In real life—airports, parking lots, kitchens, car rides, group texts. Quiet places where you either keep performing … or you finally exhale.

I learned that being a man who is comfortable with himself and easy to be around isn't about becoming firmer and more rigid. It's about becoming calmer—and knowing when less is more. It's regulated strength at the right emotional frequency.

Soft Eyes = presence that makes people feel safe.

Strong Spine = steadiness that keeps you from folding.

Together they are a framework of warmth and boundaries, that's the concept we'll live inside here. A life that feels richer, deeper, more meaningful. Pride and dignity without the armor. Real connection with your kids, friends, and romantic partners.

We'll use real-life stories you can feel in your body. This is a book about returning to yourself without the noise. If you're exhausted, that makes sense. It means you've been carrying too much. If you're angry, I get it. If you're numb, I get that too.

We're not going to pretend any of it didn't happen. We're just going to build a different signal. Quietly. One notch at a time.

Take a breath. This isn't a race. It's a return.

A Note on the Way This Book Moves

This book isn't built like a lecture. It's built like real life: a story, a moment where the air in the room changed, and a small correction you can actually use the next time your nervous system wants to sprint.

Each chapter moves the same way. I start with a story—what happened, the way it actually happened. Somewhere inside it, there's a shift: the moment the room changed, the grip loosened, the signal settled. And at the end, there are a few lines you can carry into real life.

You can read this book in order, but you don't have to. Start where something feels familiar. Skip ahead. Circle back.

These chapters are meant to work like resets, not lessons.

If you're a father, keep this in mind: Your kids don't just remember what you said. They remember what it felt like to be near you while you said it. A clean line—delivered without heat—becomes inheritance.

A quick note on the texture:

- I write in second person a lot ("you"). That's on purpose. It keeps you in the room with me.
- Field Notes appear when something needs to be named and held still for a moment.
- You're the main character here. My story is just the map.

I use humor, sarcasm, and pop culture references. That's just me trying to keep you awake. I don't pretend to be flawless. If anything, I show you exactly where the crack is.

Read slowly. Let things land. And if you can't remember the last time you exhaled all the way … you're in the right place.

PART I

THE NOISE

Most men don't lose their families in one dramatic moment. They lose them through a thousand small settings they never chose. The volume creeps up. The pace gets frantic. The body stays on alert. You start living like every conversation is a situation you have to manage.

Noise isn't just sound. It's the internal static that tells you you're behind, you're failing, you're about to get blamed. It's the feeling that if you don't stay on top of everything—tone, schedule, money, discipline, the story—everything will slide. So you tighten. You speak faster. You correct more. You try to steer the room with force.

This part is the "before" photo. Not to shame you. To name what's real. Because if you can't see the pattern, you'll keep defending it like it's your personality. A lot of men confuse intensity for care. They think heat equals leadership. They think pressure equals protection. And then they wonder why the house feels like it's always unsettled.

You'll meet the version of me who meant well and still made things worse. You'll see how the wrong emotional speed can turn ordinary life into a constant argument with reality. And you'll start noticing your own tells—the moments you tighten, the moments you rush, the moments you push when what you really want is connection.

The noise isn't your identity. It's a setting. And settings can change.

The First Quiet Moment

Awakening doesn't announce itself. It doesn't arrive with answers or certainty or a clear plan. Most of the time, it shows up as a half-second pause where you notice your own body before you rush past it.

That's where this story actually begins. Not with the divorce. Not with a diagnosis. Not with the moment everyone else would point to and say, "There. That's it."

It begins in a house at night, when the noise finally drops low enough for a man to catch himself in a mirror and realize something simple and unsettling. I'm still stiffening even now. That recognition isn't failure. It's the first opening.

LOOKING IN THE MIRROR

The First Honest Look

The mirror is a mean thing because it never lies. And when you're a divorced guy in his late fifties, the mirrors seem to multiply. They're not just the ones in airports or gyms, or the ones in hotel bathrooms with the unforgiving LED lights. They're the quick hits you don't ask for: your face in harsh light, the softening you can't argue with, the tiredness you can't charm away.

The worst one is the one in your own house, late at night. The one you catch for half a second while brushing your teeth. The one you see from across the room when you're lying in bed, staring at the ceiling, wondering who the hell you are now.

You know the exact mirror I mean. Not the dramatic one where you stare yourself down like Rocky before the fight. The regular one. Sink. Toothbrush. That soft hum of a house at night when the kids are finally down and you're moving through rooms like you don't want to wake the past.

Sometimes I'd catch my own eyes in that glass and feel my body doing what it had been trained to do for decades—tighten … scan … lock up. It wasn't always a thought. Half the time it was just a grip in my jaw, a little pressure behind my ribs, a quiet readiness like something bad might be right around the corner, waiting for me to miss it.

And that's the part the mirror shows you when you're not posing for anybody. Not your smile. Not your story. Your frequency.

Divorce shifts the geometry of a man's life. It tilts the floorboards. It distorts the acoustics of every room you walk into. It fills your head with a mix of confusion, relief, shame, anger, hope, and whatever emotion shows up next in the emotional lottery. But the loudest worry, the one almost no divorced dad says out loud, is simple: How do I keep my relationship with my kids alive?

You don't want to lose ground. You don't want to miss a chance. You don't want your kids to think the divorce means their dad is only half there.

And when a man starts fearing that, he spirals. He overthinks everything. He imagines disaster scenarios. He rewrites conversations in his head. He convinces himself one wrong text will break something fragile.

That's when your nervous system becomes a kind of internal weather radar: constantly scanning, constantly anticipating, constantly clenching.

How Your Body Tells on You

I didn't need a therapist to diagnose me. I started to recognize a pattern in my wiring. Even now, the same triggers can still light up that need to make a correction—real, immediate.

It's the feeling I get on a long, high bridge, or an overpass with water on both sides. Something in my nervous system misfires. I've felt it my whole life, even before I had words for it. Not panic. Not terror. Just a sudden narrowing of the world, like someone dimmed the edges.

My brain goes into hyper-focus: eyes on the vanishing point, hands gripping, breath turning shallow, body bracing for the "don't swerve" moment. I get so focused on not drifting toward the right edge that my hands forget how to be hands for a minute.

I ease into the middle lane like it's a life raft and talk myself through it like a guy defusing a bomb. Not fear of the bridge collapsing. Not fear of death. Fear of my own mistake.

The fear of fucking up—Lack of Control's dominant personality trait. It morphs into a very specific adult fear: loss-of-control vertigo. It shows up in places with:

- No exits
- No space
- No agency
- No ability to fix anything
- No room for error

It is the reason that the high bridges freak me out so much. It is the same reason my heart spikes whenever I watch a Philadelphia Eagles game and see their famous "Tush Push" move at the goal line. The play is really pretty boring, but what makes my chest tighten is feeling the helplessness that big, tough center who hiked the ball has to endure while he is buried under bodies. As they slowly peel off one 300-pound man after another, he can only sit still and wait. He can't use his strength or all the techniques he has learned. For that moment he is utterly helpless, waiting on the world around him to return to his normal.

It's the same reason that you feel helpless in that few minutes between the plane stopping at your gate and the plane door opening. It is only a few minutes, and it always ends the same way. The door opens and people get off. However that moment of inability to make any corrections would tickle my insides in the wrong way.

There are the fears men admit out loud. And then there are the quieter ones—the strange, body-level jolts that make no logical sense, the ones we hide because we don't even know how to explain them. This fear I finally was able to start to see is one of those.

Some men fear heights. Some fear closed spaces. Some fear drowning. Some fear the dark. But my fear has always been different—subtle, odd, and almost embarrassing to describe. Not fear of dying. Not fear of crashing. Not fear of catastrophe. My fear is simpler: "What if I lose control for one second?" It's about agency—the moment in life when your body whispers: "Please don't let me make a mistake."

The MRI That Said the Quiet Part Out Loud

As you age, things that never crossed your mind start to become noticeable. For me, it was this continual rumbling in my left ear. Turns out it was a form of tinnitus. No big deal. I figured it would be resolved with a normal doctor's visit, some tests, maybe a prescription and the doctor telling me there was something I shouldn't do any longer. It was surprising when he returned and told me, "We don't normally do an MRI for this, but we want to check to be sure no abnormalities show up when we scan your head."

Next, it was forty minutes in a tube the size of a coffin. A cage over my head. A technician asking, "Are you claustrophobic?" That was when it actually started to hit me. This long fear I had been holding my entire life. I laughed it off like a guy pretending not to be nervous on a first date. As they slid me into the chamber, I told myself to stay calm. Closed my eyes. Clutched the emergency clicker like it was the last rope on a cliff.

Halfway through, they slid me out—not to save me, just to readjust something—and when they pushed me back in, something ancient fired off inside my ribs that was all too familiar.

Don't lose control. Not now. Not here. This wasn't panic. This wasn't fear of death. This wasn't my body screaming "danger." It was the one fear men like me know too well. The terror of being pinned with no way to steer. I don't fear disaster. I fear being conscious and unable to move—trapped in the suspended second before impact.

Every man with this wiring shares the same truth. You're not afraid of dying. You're afraid of dying helpless. That's not fragility. It's not panic. It's not a flaw.

It's the framework of a lifetime where you are the regulator, the guy who steadies the ship. A lifetime of holding things together, staying rational, anticipating danger, managing emotion, absorbing impact, leaves very little room for surrender. So the moments where surrender is required? Your system spikes. Not because you're weak but because you're overtrained. The bridges, the MRI, the Tush Push, the plane exit, they are similar but different, and each gripping.

Soft Eyes, Strong Spine starts with noticing the stiffening … and learning you can let it release without the world falling apart. When I was in my twenties and thirties and forties, there were no books that explained this. As I started to drift out of my fifties, I realized that there should be a book to help dads like me navigate life.

It's a book that can be a North Star, a shining light showing us that we are not alone. There are millions and millions of us fathers that want to be there, want to be present, want to be the best father they can. This is a calm in the storm. A long exhale. A place you can stand for a minute without needing to fix anything.

Hello, My Name Is

My name is Eric Brockman. I'm a twice-divorced guy in his late fifties, father to four extraordinary kids, and someone who pays the bills by selling composite materials to aerospace and defense companies. It's not glamorous work, but it's honest, and it's taken me all over the country and to many places around the world.

I'd love to say I'm a flawless dad, but the truth is more complicated. I've always been involved. I've always tried hard. I've always shown up. I've always loved my kids. But trying hard isn't the same as being emotionally available in the ways your kids actually need at the moments they need it.

If I'm honest with myself (and this book doesn't work if I'm not), I'm doing well with two of my kids, I'm rebuilding a relationship with another, and I've been estranged from one for years. Writing that sentence still knots my stomach. But honesty is the only way any of this matters.

I didn't set out to write a book. I was just trying to stay

standing. Life had gotten louder than I could keep up with—raising boys, losing a marriage, holding too much at work, trying to keep everyone else calm while I quietly braced for impact. If you're a man who's ever carried more than he could say out loud, you already know the weight I'm talking about.

For most of my life, I thought strength meant gripping harder—more responsibility, more vigilance, more readiness to fix whatever might go wrong. It worked … until it didn't.

Somewhere in the middle of airports, kitchens, empty driveways, and silent nights thinking about my kids (especially my daughter, who went quiet for a long season), something in me cracked open. Not dramatically, but quietly. A shift so subtle I almost missed it.

I learned that strength has less to do with pulling tight and more to do with letting go of the grip. That presence matters more than performance. That my kids didn't need a superhero; they needed a steady man with a calm center. That life stops feeling like a fight the moment you stop treating it like one.

This is a book about fixing yourself. It's the story of how one man finally learned to show up in his own life without bracing for impact, and what changed when he did.

You won't find perfection here. You will find honesty. You'll find the moments that broke me open and the moments that put me back together, one conversation, one car ride, one quiet breath at a time.

If you are a father, you'll find yourself in these pages. If you are a man, you'll recognize the old wiring. If you are rebuilding anything—your identity, your family, your confidence—you'll see that the path forward is not force but steadiness.

The entire book comes down to a simple idea. Soft Eyes, the

presence that makes people feel safe. Strong Spine, the steadiness that keeps you from folding.

I didn't learn this quickly. I learned it slowly, painfully, finally. If any part of your life feels loud right now, or heavy, or uncertain, we start here, quietly.

Take a breath. Set the book down if you need to. Come back when you can. This isn't a race. It's a return. Welcome.

When the Settings Got Built

Most men think their story starts with divorce, or a breaking point, or the moment life finally screams loud enough that they can't ignore it. It doesn't.

Every man begins with settings he didn't choose: childhood wiring, roles assigned quietly, lessons learned without anyone speaking them aloud. Before we get to any of my stories, we have to go back to the boy who learned to carry things without ever saying he was carrying them. For me, that boy showed up in a red satin jacket.

The youth football team I played on in Sharon was called the Red Devils. And every kid in my small town knew what the real Red Devils jacket looked like. Shiny 80s red body and sleeves, white piping, that heavier weight you felt when you shrugged into it. And up on the chest, the detail that mattered almost as much as the team name: the BIKE logo.

Before Nike ate the world, BIKE was the brand for team jackets. If you had the BIKE version, you weren't just on the team, you were in it.

When my mother agreed to get me one, she drove me to Marciano's Sporting Goods in Mansfield Center. Even the store carried its own myth—Marciano, like Rocky Marciano, the undefeated heavyweight champ from Brockton a couple towns over. Where I grew up, even your sporting-goods store carried a story.

We walked in, me buzzing with that particular kind of seventh-grade electricity. Old enough to know what status is, young enough to believe a jacket could grant it. We found the rack, the color, the cut. And then we hit the problem.

Whether it was timing, money, inventory, or just the luck of the draw, Marciano's didn't have the BIKE jacket in my size. What they had was something close, an off-brand shell that resembled the real one if you didn't look too hard.

To their credit, they tried to make it right. They got the Red Devils/Hockomock League patch. They stitched it on carefully. Then they put my name on the sleeve, the unmistakable signature of those jackets.

On paper, I had the thing. But if you were a kid who paid attention, you saw the gaps. The striping wasn't quite the same. The lettering on my sleeve didn't match that on the BIKE version. The fabric felt lighter.

The whole thing lived in that space between almost right and not quite. None of this was anyone's fault. My mother was doing her best. Marciano's was doing their best. This wasn't neglect, this was New England, middle-class make it work. Inside me, though, something registered.

I smiled. Said nothing. Shrugged into the jacket like it was perfect. Not because I didn't see the differences, but because the safest thing, even then, was to not make a fuss. This is how wiring gets laid down in real time.

Don't complain. Don't ask for more. Take what you're given and adapt. Make everyone else's life easier. Shrink just enough that no one feels bad. That quiet instinct became the beginning of something I wouldn't name until decades later. Eric 1.0—the version of me that learns to carry disappointment alone so no one else has to feel it.

The jacket kept me warm. It had the right patch. It said "Red Devils" and "Hockomock League" in all the right places. But I learned a lesson wearing it that stuck longer than any fabric ever could: Sometimes the easiest way to move through the world is to swallow the difference and pretend everything fits.

And it wasn't just clothes. The house itself taught that same lesson: handle it quietly, leave the evidence, keep moving.

The house had its own weathering, the kind you stop seeing because they become part of the architecture. One of them lived under the kitchen sink. I can still picture the cabinet door: the inside top section charred black, the burn irregular and circular in places—as if the wood had caught unevenly, flaring here and fading there. It wasn't dramatic. It wasn't a headline. It was just there—this small, permanent "something happened here."

The night it happened, I didn't wake to yelling. We kids didn't know about it until the next day or so. There wasn't an odd smell or a big scene. Everything was matter-of-fact.

In my head, I can picture the scene. My father—bare feet on the kitchen floor, moving with that quiet certainty he had when something needed doing. He didn't flip on every light and announce the emergency. He didn't turn it into a family meeting.

He just found the source like a man who had done it before: a trash bag pressed too close, an ashtray dumped from the night before, a hidden ember, a corner that got hotter than it should've. He pulled it out, smothered it, got water where water needed to go. Contained. Finished.

My mother coming in halfway through, hair up, eyes not fully open. She takes a look at the cabinet, looks at him, and an agreement passes between them without a single word. We're okay. Tomorrow still exists. Then she went back to bed.

By morning, it was already becoming furniture. No one gathered us. No one explained. The trash can moved. The cabinet stayed burned. Life went on with the same tone it always had. That was a setting. Something flares. Someone handles it. We don't linger. And when you grow up inside that rhythm, you learn to treat heat like a private matter.

A few years later, my sister and I found a can of Coke in the fridge—rare enough back then to feel like we were holding contraband. We shook it because we were kids and the whole point of being a kid is testing how much fun you can have before the rules show up.

We popped it open in the kitchen and the ceiling took the hit. Brown spray. Sticky freckles. A sudden little rainstorm of sugar and rebellion. For a second we froze, watching it drip like it might confess on us. My mother stood there, took it in, and sighed. Not sharp. Not cruel. Not theatrical. Just the sound of someone doing the math on energy.

She wiped what she could reach. The rest—up high, out of reach—stayed. She wasn't ignoring it; she was keeping it from becoming a whole thing. And here's the part that matters: it stayed without becoming a character flaw.

Years later you could still see those faint brown ghosts up on the ceiling if the light hit right. People would notice sometimes. A guest's eyes would track upward. That half second of silence where somebody decides whether to ask a question. And my mother would smile and say, "My kids were the interior decorators."

She made it light. She made it normal. She made it small enough to fit inside a laugh instead of a shame spiral. The marks became part of the room. Evidence that mess didn't have to become a crisis. Proof that a family could absorb a flare-up without turning the volume to ten.

I didn't know I was learning anything. I thought I was just watching adults be adults. But that kitchen taught me two things that lived deep in the wiring:

Problems didn't need witnesses.

And the cleanup didn't require an audience.

Once you learn a house can burn a little without anybody raising their voice, you start sniffing for smoke in every room before you even step inside it.

The Invisible Audience

Once a kid learns to shrink, he also learns to scan. Not dramatically. Not in a way a teacher would ever spot. It's quieter than that. It's internal. It happens in the beat between entering a room and taking your first step inside it.

You read the temperature. You read the energy. You read the possibility of something going wrong even when nothing ever does.

Long before anyone made *The Truman Show*, my mind had already written a low-budget version. I'd be on my paper route in fourth grade, or wandering the playground, and I'd get this feeling that there was a studio audience somewhere watching me.

I can still see one of the earliest versions of it like it's a scene from an old VHS tape. Fourth grade. Paper route mornings. That quiet, lonely hour where the neighborhood feels like it hasn't fully decided to wake up yet.

My mind would drift and, no joke, it was like there was a little studio booth somewhere, a camera crew, a director, somebody watching me. Not mocking. Not cruel. More like: "Just don't do anything dumb, Brockman."

Sometimes the "person in the booth" was a girl from school, Betty Holly—purple crayon energy, Donny Osmond posters, the kind of childhood crush that never even gets spoken out loud. She once put a purple crayon in the pencil sharpener. I still remember it because it felt like the most rebellious thing a person could do at nine years old.

Other times it was just a nameless audience. A cool song would hit on my Walkman and I'd imagine the booth people nodding like, yeah, that's a good one.

Even now, as an adult, I'll catch a whiff of it while watering a yard, messing with a hose, doing something normal. I'll feel a faint sense that a neighbor might be watching, so I should look calm, cool, and like I've got it handled. It's not paranoia. It's early appeasement.

It's the first training in being "okay" in public … even when they don't know what you're doing in private. Better not trip. Better not pick your nose. Better not be the kid who looks like he doesn't belong. It sounds odd written out, but that's how early tuning works.

You start living as if someone is always watching, and your private goal becomes simple. Don't screw this up for anyone. Walking across a playground? You give yourself instructions.

Don't say anything stupid. Don't draw attention. Don't be the problem.

Over at a friend's house? You're checking for signs you're overstaying your welcome. Family gatherings? You're the one smoothing the edges, noticing who's irritated, who's tired, who's close to snapping, and adjusting yourself accordingly.

From the outside, you look like the good kid. The polite kid. The one who "doesn't need much." The one teachers love because you never cause trouble. Inside, you're running a 24/7 emotional operations center no one else can see. A private weather channel, broadcasting only to you. And that's where the mask forms. Not as dishonesty. As responsibility.

You become the easy kid. The quiet kid. The no-needs kid. The one who adapts, absorbs, adjusts. People praise you for it. Adults reward you for it. You don't know it yet, but you're building the operating system you'll carry into adulthood and into fatherhood. Once that mask sets in childhood? It takes decades to even realize it exists.

The Outlaw Bookseller

There was one place we would go. My dad's best friend's house, which had a pool. They used to live on our street but got a bigger house when I was young. My dad went by "Tom" to most people, but he was "Boy" to Mark. Two guys who could make any day feel like a holiday.

The pool had its own weather. The smell of chlorine, the slap of wet feet on concrete. A big cassette stereo box running non-stop, loud enough to carry over the water all afternoon. His wife,

Linda, was in charge of the stereo. She was one of the warmest people I ever had the pleasure to know.

The pool had people of all ages coming and going like it was a public park, except it was better because Mark was there and he made it feel like you belonged the second you walked through the gate.

He ran his rare-book business out of the basement of that house. When he moved in and started it, my mom, Helen, went to work for him.

Mark was a character. He dealt in old, rare, collectible, historically significant books, plus maps, prints, manuscripts. His lane was Western Americana. It sounds narrow until you realize he wasn't small-time. At his funeral, people keep repeating: he could look at a book and know, instantly, if it was a "buy it" or a "piece of shit."

That was Mark. Over the years he leaned into a Western look—cowboy boots, jeans, a cigarette hanging off his mouth, a black Rolling Stones T-shirt, and a green satin Baylor jacket. Weather didn't matter. The boots and the jacket showed up anyway.

He had games. One was called "Sak a Hawi," which sounds ridiculous on the page, but in real life it was loud and competitive and exactly the kind of nonsense that makes a boy feel rich. But the best one was "Off the House." He'd made it up from scratch when he had extra tennis balls lying around from the next door neighbor's tennis court.

We'd line up and take shots at the house. For real, at his house. We all did it. The rules were half sport and half mythology. Nine innings, three outs a side, mostly baseball. If the ball hit the drainpipe, it was a home run. If it clipped the edge of the gutter and fell in just right, it was also a home run. The wall by the laundry room and the kids' playroom was a double. Mark would argue like a trial lawyer. My dad would jump in and argue like a man who knew he was wrong but enjoyed the fight anyway.

Linda was the referee. She'd sit in a chair under the umbrella or lie under the throwing lane in her lounge chair. As needed, she would chime in and settle all disputes with a look that made grown men immediately behave. One rule everyone knew: "Don't jump into the birch tree!"

And that's the part I didn't understand at the time: Mark wasn't just a guy with a fun house and a pool and a good game. He was a second set of adult hands on the wheel for me. Not in a dramatic way. In the quiet way that matters. An extra man in the orbit who saw me, knew my dad, and didn't require a performance.

So yeah, I still learned to scan. I still learned to be the easy kid. But in that backyard, for a few hours at a time, the booth light went off. No audience. No grading. Just a boy, a towel, and grown men laughing like they had invented summer.

Humor as Camouflage

Somewhere along the way I discovered humor. Real humor. Boston humor. Dry. Sideways. Slightly off-center. My mom and dad both grew up in nearby areas of Boston and carried that with them. So growing up we all knew the kind of humor where you can always laugh at yourself or others. At first, humor was just something I had. Then it became something I used.

I learned that a well-timed line could change the temperature of a room. If tension started to rise, I'd crack something. If silence got awkward, I'd fill it. If someone was simmering, I'd redirect. If I felt exposed, I'd aim the joke at myself.

Over time, I realized something important: I didn't become the funny kid, I became the safe kid. If everyone was laughing, no one was breaking. If the room stayed light, no one was looking too closely. If I could keep you smiling, you wouldn't fall, and if you didn't fall, I didn't have to brace for impact.

Humor is a hell of a tool at ten. It works even better at twenty. By thirty, it's almost invisible. But there's a side effect most men don't notice until much later. You can get so good at keeping everything light that you forget how to let anything be true.

That's where 1.0 gets sneaky. It looks like confidence, but it's camouflage. It looks like charm, but it's temperature control. It looks like connection, but it's actually protection. And when you don't know you're hiding, you don't know how to stop.

FIELD NOTES
The Physics of Fog

Fog forms when warm air meets cold resistance

Emotional fog forms when a man wired

for connection lives in patterns wired for

unpredictability

You adjust, you anticipate, you over-function

Fog is not failure, it's physics

Florida, The First Frequency Mismatch

Moving to Florida wasn't part of some grand life plan. It was survival. It was a young couple with two new degrees—mechanical engineering for me, childhood education for my first wife—trying to make something work in the middle of a brutal 1991 job market.

If you weren't around then, trust me: 1991 was a hiring freeze wrapped inside a recession wrapped inside a shrug from every HR department in New England.

The pitch was simple. She could get a teaching job down south. I'd figure out the engineering thing once we got settled. We were in love, and young enough to believe that love was a strategy. And we had my Uncle Paul, a legendary character in my life, anchored down in Port St. Lucie.

Paul moved to Florida in the late '60s and built his life from scratch. He finished pharmacy school, took a job with one of the big chains, and saved enough to open his own place—Riverview Pharmacy. A mom-and-pop by design, it succeeded beyond anything he'd imagined. Eventually, he sold it back to the system he'd once worked inside. A full-circle success.

I'm telling you about him now because he was one of the first men I watched build something solid from the ground up. Back then, I didn't have words for it—I just felt how steady it was.

Later, Uncle Paul got sick—not suddenly, but slowly. Early in that stretch, I'd get one last good day with him—me, my boys, and Paul out on the ocean fishing, the kind of day that still lives in a photograph.

He was thinner and tired that day, but unmistakably himself.

Present. Still inhabiting his life instead of managing it. At the time, I didn't name what I was noticing. I just filed it away.

Near the end, I was there. I held his hand and told him I loved him, that he had always been good to me.

The Big Three and the Birth of Introspection

When he died, I went to the funeral carrying a version of myself I believed was solid. Functional. Responsible. The kind of man who can carry weight and keep moving. Sitting in that service, listening to people talk about Paul—the risks he took, the way he showed up, the way he stayed alive even as his body failed—something quiet but undeniable surfaced in me.

At some point, I remember thinking it in plain English. My big three—Paul, Tom, and Mark—were all gone. It wasn't grief exactly. It was recognition. A clear sense that I had been looking at my own life through the wrong lenses for a long time.

Paul's death didn't teach me anything new. It did something more uncomfortable than that. It stripped away my ability to keep pretending I didn't already know. I could see the gap between a life that is merely endured and one that is actually inhabited.

I could feel how much of myself I had been holding, performing, managing, and how little of myself I had been present for. This wasn't my father's death all over again. That loss belonged to an earlier version of me.

This one landed differently, quieter, slower. It didn't change my life overnight. There were long stretches afterward where nothing visibly shifted at all. But it marked the first time I understood that the work ahead of me wasn't about fixing anything that was broken. It was about replacing the lenses I had been using to see myself, my relationships, and the kind of man I was becoming.

This is the moment my introspective journey truly begins. What began as journaling, a way to release the feelings and capture all the thoughts and notes I had gathered over the years, grew into something larger. I wanted to capture this fundamental shift I was observing, experiencing, and living.

The writing was primarily created as an artifact for my kids, but as the thoughts and insights started to pour out, I realized this was more than just a memoir of stories for my kids. More than a few notable learnings. This was a shift in how someone can live their life.

Concepts that appear vague and hard to grasp start to become intuitively obvious when you synthesize them to nugget-size bits and write them down. That's what this book is. What I wanted to have twenty years ago.

But these books don't exist, and the reason they don't exist is the audience. Divorced men. We're a bunch of bumbling dads trying to manage whatever fragile relationship is left with our kids. No matter how strong the bond was before the divorce, it will get tested.

We don't pick up books to adjust a lens and look deep into the mirror, because we have been trained on a toxic form of masculinity. One that prevents emotional connections. If you allow yourself to go there, this book will break those old conventions.

My uncle's death was that launching point for me. Because of the man he was and the man he would want me to be. That is why we start the book with Paul and Florida.

Titusville and NASA

Back to my story and the move to Florida, which was a bumpy ride. We landed in Vero Beach first, staying in a double-wide trailer owned by my first wife's grandmother. They were generous and treated us well, but it wasn't luxury accommodations. One afternoon, she had to go chase the cable company just to get it hooked up.

To her credit, she found a job as a fourth-grade teacher in Titusville, and we moved into an apartment down there. It was our first place. Not glamorous—just a standard Titusville third-floor walkup on Route 1—but it felt like enough. Even got a beagle we called "Chumley."

Lenny, another "uncle," this one connected to NASA, got me a list of every subcontractor within shouting distance of a launchpad. No email back then. Just phone calls and envelopes. Helen (my mom) became my personal OfficeMax. I'd call her constantly with new names and leads. She'd print my resume on that cream-colored "professional" paper, tuck it into the matching envelope, and send it out. I'd follow up wherever I could—HR departments, receptionists, whoever would take the call. Knock. Wait. Hope. Repeat.

Substitute teaching came somewhere in the middle—forty-five bucks a day, tie and Dockers, trying to pass as someone who had it together. My first assignment was a middle school math class, where I walked into a live boxing match between two eighth-grade girls who'd clearly studied Hagler–Hearns the night before.

My Boston accent came out full force: "Get outta he-ah!" And somehow, the room snapped into order. Some careers begin with precision. Mine began with a fistfight and a cheap tie.

Finally, I landed interviews with EG&G—a Boston-based company, of all things. I wore my one suit, cranked the AC in the car so high the windshield fogged over, and played adult. First interview. Then a second. Then an offer—followed almost immediately by a hiring freeze.

But the shuttle launches were still there. In that season, they were everything. Day launches were spectacular. Night launches were something else. You don't just watch a night launch—you feel it.

There was one February launch I'll never forget. The kind that drags on with delays until it's practically morning. Cold for central Florida—low forties. Crowds gathered in parking lots up and down Route 1, headlights off, people standing outside their cars like we were waiting for a sermon. We watched from our balcony, our dog already wedged under the bed. He hated the sonic booms.

When the shuttle finally lit, it was light, yes. Sound, yes. But it was temperature, too. A wash of warmth rolled over us from behind, like someone had rolled a giant space heater up to our backs.

And then the sequence reversed as cleanly as a switch. Cold to warm. Dark to lit. Roar to something that felt like it might carry us with it. Then, as it climbed and the engines throttled down: Warmth, gone. Light, fading. Sound, thinning to silence. Cold again.

I didn't know it then, but that night would give me a pattern I'd recognize later—the first decade of my adulthood in miniature. A sudden lift, a flash of hope, a surge of energy, and then everything goes cold again.

Florida wasn't a failure. It was an origin story. It was where I first learned I could misread the emotional frequency of a moment so badly that I'd pull two lives out of Florida and back north—choosing logic and potential over presence and truth.

Florida gave me a thousand small lessons I wasn't yet mature enough to name. The biggest one? You can be doing all the "right" things on paper and still be tuned to the wrong frequency.

Lebanon, Potential, and the Cost of Not Sitting Still

From Florida, I talked my first wife into moving to Lebanon, New Hampshire. On the surface, it made perfect sense. My best man in that first wedding had landed a job there at a small environmental products company.

The Upper Valley had beautiful mountains and real seasons—an actual winter that felt good after the Florida humidity. My engineering degree would finally line up with a real job. That's what I told myself. Underneath, the truth was simpler:

I didn't know how to sit with stillness. I didn't know how to hold uncertainty. I didn't know how to be honest about fear. So I did what over-functioning men do—I converted discomfort into logistics.

New town. New job. New plan. New move. We went, made some good friends. The people were great. But in the end, pretty humbling. And short-lived. The marriage didn't make it. There were a thousand reasons, and all of them were human. She had her wiring. I had mine. Neither of us had the lens we have now.

What I didn't realize then but can see with absolute clarity now is that one of the quiet superpowers of *Soft Eyes, Strong Spine* is the way it teaches a man to shift perspectives without losing himself.

You learn to see your own position clearly and, at the same time, sense the emotional frequency of the moment. Most of us weren't wired for that. Our early settings were built for protection, not perception. It is what blocks us from being truly honest with ourselves. But the truth holds: The more angles a man can feel a moment from, the better choices he makes.

I didn't have that skill at twenty-three. I was all spine, no softness. Or I was all softness with no spine. All drive, no attunement. All frequency, no calibration.

Trying to live your life based solely on potential is like eating filet mignon every night—you lose the taste for it. You start craving something simpler. Something real. I didn't know it yet, but the bill for all that potential was about to come due in a way that would shape the rest of my life.

The Day My Father Died

Tom was a salesman his whole life. Out of his car. Sixty-five thousand miles—more, some years—zig-zagging eastern Massachusetts, southern New Hampshire, anywhere he could find a yes. He sold paper goods the last twenty years to restaurants. Takeout containers for Chinese food, pizza boxes, sub wraps: anything in a local fast food place that wasn't food.

He wasn't "organized" the way organized people mean it, but he had his own system. A cup of Red Rose tea at the perfect temperature. A bowl of Rice Chex with raisins. The morning newspaper with four little check marks in the business section—the hot leads for the day. He'd fold up the paper and head out the door.

He could make anybody feel comfortable. Gift of gab, timing, warmth. And he had these little quirks that become obvious only when you're close: rubbing his hands sometimes like a nervous habit, a small white towel nearby to wipe his mustache, the way a single word could mean five different things, depending on tone.

He also had a language. He'd drop a random *'is* into words like it made perfect sense:

Diet Coke became D'is C'is.
Town Spa (his beloved pizza) became T'is Sp'is.
A screwdriver, the drink or the tool, was a Scr'is Dr'is

And then there were the classics he said all the time that everyone knew by heart:

"Does a chicken have lips?"
"Say boy."
"Pleasure."

Those lines were never just lines. And we still really don't know if a chicken has lips. But it was how he said: I'm here. I'm with you. Relax. Life's heavy; let's make it lighter for a minute. That's important, because when a man like that disappears suddenly, the silence hits different.

The Day the Lens Cracked

I was thirty-two when the phone call came. Old enough to have a mortgage, a career, obligations, the outline of an adult identity … but still young enough to believe real life couldn't just walk in and flip the table.

My father, Tom, was doing what he had always done in December—helping the paper warehouse count year-end inventory. All the sales guys did it. No one liked it, but it was part of the culture, an annual ritual to prove you were still part of the team, even if you spent most of the year on the road.

He was good at that world. He had the laugh, the charm, the timing. He was the original Brockman in full bloom. And then he was gone. No slow decline. No warning signs. No doctor's speech.

Just a massive *crack*, we were told, when a homemade cherry picker platform snapped and dropped him to his death. One moment he was counting paper boxes, likely cracking jokes. The next, someone was shouting his name.

Sudden loss doesn't feel sudden. It feels unreal. Then unfair. Then like something inside you just signed a contract you never saw coming. By the time we reached the hospital, the outcome was already written.

The nurses handed us his things—his watch, his wallet, and the coat he always wore that time of year. A worn navy puffy parka, the kind of jacket New England men keep for decades without ever calling it "outerwear." It was just his coat.

I don't know why I reached into the pockets. Maybe I thought I'd find a receipt, loose change, a pen. Something normal. Instead, my fingers hit a folded piece of paper. Soft at the edges. A bit worn from being opened and refolded.

I pulled it out. It was a small sheet of paper with the handwritten lineup he was working on for the Pro Bowl for the Greater

Boston Football League (GBFL), the goofy fantasy league carried over by my brother-in-law from Chicago in the late nineties that we still play today. The new generations, including my son, are in the league now.

But this was the first year of the GBFL. That first year the league was our private universe. Dad would call at all times to talk fantasy. There were not the endless shows on TV and podcasts like today. A hot nugget he heard on the radio, like a reporter from St. Louis talking about a Marshall Faulk injury, was cause for an immediate phone call from him on his flip phone.

The league took on a life of its own. There were arguments and at one point even a mutiny, and they threw out the old commissioner and made me "The Commish."

The league became my dad's favorite thing to brag about. He knew everyone in the league, and most were family of some type that first year. So when we ended up playing each other in the first-ever championship, it was special.

It was old-school versus new-school, father against son. I won, but I know he didn't care—he may have been rooting for me.

The week after the championship game was the Pro Bowl. That's why it hit so hard to see it. Right at the top, in his crisp all-caps block-letter handwriting, was one unmistakable word:

MANNING

I just stood there. Not crying. Not collapsing. Just … stopped. There's a specific kind of silence that comes when grief intersects with something intimate and unexpected. It isn't loud. It isn't dramatic. It isn't even painful at first. It's recognition. This man, my father, had carried our game, our ritual, our weekly conversation right there in his jacket pocket. Not stuffed in a drawer. Not sitting on the counter. On him. Close to him.

Checked that morning before he walked into the warehouse. He must have thought about the lineup one more time. He must have planned that last play of the season. He must have felt, in that small way, connected to me. Because the lineup wasn't fantasy football. It was us.

And there's another Tom moment that lives right next to that lineup card in my head, one I didn't even realize was a "last time" until years later.

It was the Tuesday before the last weekend of games. In between the championship game and the Pro Bowl game I went to his house on Long Pine Road. Classic Boston split-level. You open the door and you can feel the TV glow coming from downstairs.

He was there at the bottom of the stairs the second I opened the door, as if he had GPS back then to follow me to the house. He looked up at me with that big wide grin he had and said something nobody else in the world could understand:

We did it!

I knew exactly what he meant. We were at the top of the GBFL fantasy league that had become our weekly ritual. Not anyone else. The two of us. Father and son sharing something that sounds small on paper but felt huge in real life.

So when Tom lit up at the bottom of the stairs like we'd just won the Super Bowl, it wasn't really about fantasy football. It was about the little father-and-son country we'd built together and the fact that, for one perfect week, we were on top.

And then the coat and the lineup and the word MANNING.

That's how life does it. It lets you have the perfect little moment, and then it turns off the lights without warning. I didn't feel like I was holding paper at that time. I felt like I was holding the last sentence of a conversation we'd been having for years. Loss collapses time. You're suddenly standing in two places at once—the moment you're in and every moment you didn't know was the last.

That is why I named the trophy that we still hand out today "The 26'er" after Tom's old team name and added an inscription "In Memory of Tom."

The Contract My Body Signed in December 2000

The drive home left me numb. My mother's house sounded wrong. People's voices came in at the wrong volume—too loud, too soft. Food tasted like cardboard. Tom was gone. Just gone. And with him went one of the last people in my life whose emotional barometer didn't demand anything of me.

Mark didn't stop being my dad's best friend just because my dad was gone. He just became something else, too: one of the only men in my life who knew me before the mask and didn't need the polished version.

He didn't offer a speech. He didn't try to make it make sense. He stayed in range. Present in the way steady men are—enough that you don't feel alone, but not so close that you have to perform your grief.

When a man suddenly loses the father he loved, without warning, something happens internally no one prepares you for. You start gripping your life so tightly you mistake the tension for strength. All the childhood settings shrink a little—stay easy, read the room, don't cause trouble—fused with something new.

If I pay enough attention, nothing else will fall. If I stay alert, nothing else will blindside us. If I carry more, everyone else can carry less. This is how men inherit responsibility, not through speeches but through sudden gaps.

I became the guy who checked the bolts twice. Who carried everyone's emotional weight. Who smoothed every rough edge. Who apologized for storms I didn't cause. Who believed deeply that if I stayed ready, nothing bad would surprise us again.

It didn't feel like fear. It felt like love. It felt like responsibility. It felt like what a man was supposed to do. But it was wiring. Old wiring. Wiring that would later shape how I married, how I parented, how I worked, and how I quietly disappeared inside my own life while looking like I had it all together.

That night in the hospital was the moment 1.0 hardened. The lifelong scanning sharpened. Over-functioning felt noble. Carrying weight felt required. Fixing emotions felt like duty. You can keep everyone afloat for years and never realize you're sinking.

It took me decades to see the flaw. Bad things don't stop happening because you tighten your muscles. You can't white-knuckle life. You can't out-think heartbreak. You can't negotiate with randomness. But at thirty-two, standing there with my father's coat in my hands and his Pro Bowl lineup in my fingers, I made a promise that my nervous system took as law. *Never again on my watch.*

That's the man my kids first met. That's the dad my marriages had to work with. That's the version of me this book will walk you out of.

What This Has to Do with Fatherhood

So why start here? Why talk about off-brand jackets from Marciano's, fake TV audiences, Florida launches, and a lineup card in a dead man's coat?

Because boys don't stay boys. They grow up. They become husbands. They become fathers. They build homes. They carry mortgages. They carry expectations. They carry whatever weight they inherited plus whatever weight they think they're supposed to carry.

And the wiring that formed at eight or twelve doesn't disappear at twenty-eight or forty-eight. It adapts. It evolves. It hides inside responsibilities that look admirable on the surface. The boy who shrank to fit a jacket becomes the man who downplays his needs. The kid who read every room becomes the man who anticipates emotions before anyone speaks. The young guy who used humor to keep the peace becomes the dad who keeps things light when they actually need to be real. The son who lost his father suddenly becomes the man who grips everything, afraid to let anything fall.

From the outside, you look like you're doing great. You're at the games. You're handling work. You're shuttling kids. You're smoothing over conflicts. You're taking the emotional hit so your kids don't have to.

People say things like, "I don't know how you do it." Inside, over time, you start to feel something different. Like you've been cast in a role—Support Beam, Emotional Buffer, The Rock—and no one remembers the man inside the part.

Here's the piece we'll keep coming back to. Your kids don't just feel your love. They feel your frequency. They feel whether you're present or performing, steady or tightened, listening or scanning. They can't always name it, but their bodies know the difference between a father who's with them and a father who's managing them.

This book exists to give you language and stories and simple, usable codes so you can keep the love and lose the clenching. So you can show up for your kids in a way that feels calm instead of corrective, present instead of pressured, soft-eyed and strong-spined the way you wish someone had shown up for you.

This isn't a story of perfection. It's a story of recalibration. Of a man waking up inside the life he built and learning how to live it differently. Of shifting from 1.0 to 2.0, not by becoming a "better" version of himself, but by becoming a clearer one. We've started with my mirror.

In the next chapter, we'll walk inside the house where all this wiring met real life and became weather.

NOTES FROM A DIVORCED DAD
What to Carry Forward

- Soft Eyes is presence that makes people feel safe—starting with the way you show up in your own body
- Strong Spine is steadiness that keeps you from folding—especially when you're scared and tempted to perform
- The mirror doesn't accuse you, it reveals your frequency

- The first shift is awareness—the moment you notice the grip
- You don't need a new life; you need a cleaner lens for the one you're in

A STORM INSIDE THE HOUSE

When the Storm Lives Indoors

If the first chapter was about the boy who learned to grip, this chapter is about the man who took that wiring into a house and tried to build a life with it.

It's one thing to carry vigilance in your chest. It's another thing to build a marriage, raise kids, and manage a home with a nervous system still tuned to "don't let anything fall."

Houses don't create your wiring. They reveal it. The front door doesn't just open into a kitchen and a living room and a hallway of bedrooms. It opens into old patterns trying to survive adult responsibilities. It opens into the parts of you that will do almost anything to keep your kids safe, your partner steady, and the fragile structure of the family from cracking.

I can picture keeping an eye on the house and feeling like the job was getting done. Today, writing this, I can see how choppy it was. As I have learned through taking deep, honest looks at myself, there were times the results didn't match the effort.

The evenings when I didn't travel and would commute back from Spartanburg, I used to enter the house like I was stepping onto a stage set I had built—and now had to perform inside. Before my shoes were even fully off, my body would start running the scan, not as a thought, but as a reflex. What's the temperature in here? What's the tone? Who's up? Is anyone irritated? Did I just walk into something I'm supposed to fix?

It's wild how fast a man can go from "home" to "operations." The kids would be somewhere in the background—a cartoon voice, a backpack thump, the sound of a cabinet—and I'd be smiling, saying the normal stuff, while my nervous system quietly moved into position like a goalie squaring up to a shot.

Not because anyone was threatening me. Because I had been trained, for decades, to believe that if something went wrong inside these walls … it would be because I missed it.

Before you can understand the fear, you have to understand the weather inside the house where all my old wiring first learned how to stay alert.

This was that house. This was that season. Not a storm anyone pointed at. Just the kind of fog that settles in quietly and teaches you to live tightened.

The Fog No One Talks About

Fog sneaks in. It doesn't announce itself with slamming doors or shattering plates or a neighbor calling the cops. It rolls in quietly, so slow, low, and confident you won't notice it at first. In our house, fog sounded like a sigh that landed half an octave lower than yesterday. A fork placed on a plate with just a little too much punctuation. A silence that had a temperature, not a topic. Or footsteps that carried mood before they carried a person.

The kitchen would be humming with normal life, the dishwasher running, a pot still warm on the stove, a kid asking what was for dinner tomorrow even though we hadn't finished tonight. On the surface, everything looked fine.

Fog also sounded like me talking too much, filling the air so no one could hear the thing underneath it. Not yelling. Not angry. Just … busy with words.

Because in my wiring, silence wasn't neutral. Silence was the hallway right before a door slams. But if you listened underneath the clatter and the cartoons and the ESPN highlight reel in the next room, there was another layer. A pressure you could feel but not name.

The fog usually arrived between 5:30 and 7:30 p.m., the witching hours of family life when everyone was home but no one was really settled yet. Homework was half-done. Backpacks were half-unzipped. Dishes were half-rinsed. Text messages were half-read.

In that window, all the unfinished pieces of the day floated through the house at once, and my nervous system did what it had always done. It scanned.

Is she okay? Are the kids okay? Did I miss something? Is tonight the night the storm finally hits?

From the outside, the scene looked like a typical suburban evening. Two working parents. Kids in various stages of adolescence. Bags and gear by the door. A calendar inside the cabinet with more ink than white space.

Inside my chest, it felt like approaching a coastline in dense fog, lights somewhere out there, horns in the distance, and the constant low-grade fear of hitting something you can't see. You don't call this a storm. You call it "being busy," "being tired," "having a lot going on." But your body knows better.

FIELD NOTES
Fog vs. Fire

Fire gets attention. Everyone sees it. Everyone agrees it's bad.

Fog is trickier. Fog gives everyone plausible deniability.

No one is yelling. No one is throwing things. No one is "abusing" anyone. Fog is how decent people can slowly lose each other without a single headline moment.

It's how a house can look normal from the street and feel heavy the second you cross the threshold. So you tell yourself everything is fine, even as your nervous system keeps quietly bracing for impact.

Fog isn't failure. Fog is physics, the warm air of good intentions hitting the cold air of unmet needs.

The Invisible Job of Being the Barometer

Along the way I took it upon myself to be the emotional barometer of the house. My wiring had already trained me to read rooms before I walked into them. I knew how to clock micro-changes in tone, volume, and pace. I felt I could scan a playground, a baseball field, or a family gathering in under five seconds and tell you who was on the verge of losing it.

In marriage, that wiring didn't go away. It just got promoted. My ex had her own history, her own wiring, her own storms she'd survived long before she met me. She wanted clarity, direction, partnership, answers she could rely on. She wanted a co-pilot, not a passenger.

I, meanwhile, had been raised to believe that the safest version of myself was the smallest one. The kid who didn't need much. The man who could absorb a lot. If you recall, I had this weird little childhood thing that felt like *The Truman Show* years before the movie existed.

When tension rose in the house, I did what my wiring knew. I scanned. I adjusted. I pulled back, not out of coldness but out of habit. Out of fear of "getting it wrong." Out of not wanting to escalate anything.

I'd walk into the kitchen, clock the exact angle of a shoulder, the way a cabinet door closed, the half-second delay before "Hey" came out, and my internal dashboard would light up. Storm front, pressure dropping, visibility low.

There was a simple Tuesday night at Dunkin', one of our usual drive-thru stops between swim, baseball practice, and home, when we got our goodies and pulled back into traffic, and I heard a cabinet close two rooms away inside my head.

Not in the house. In my body. That's the level of conditioning we're talking about. Your nervous system doesn't wait for external confirmation. It runs simulations twenty-four hours a day. Is there a fight coming? Is the weekend about to blow up? Is this one of those nights where the kids feel it, even if no one says a word?

The cruel thing about being the barometer is that the better you get at it, the less anyone realizes you're doing it. From the outside, you look calm. From the outside, you look steady. From the outside, you look like the guy who "never makes a big deal."

Inside, you're managing pressure systems no one else can see.

The Storm No One Sees but the Kids Feel

Kids are better meteorologists than we give them credit for. They don't have the language for "emotional barometer" or "relational fog," but their bodies know when the pressure changes.

They hear how something is said. They feel when a hug is a half-second shorter. They notice which rooms get quieter when two adults pass each other in the hallway and say, "Hey," like it's a complete conversation.

My kids were growing up inside that house. They saw a dad who was present at games, at concerts, at the dinner table. They also felt a dad whose nervous system never fully dropped out of a defensive crouch. That's the thing about tensing: You can hide it with a smile, but you can't hide it from the people who live with you. They feel your frequency even when they like your jokes.

I remember one night standing in the doorway, watching one of the boys brush his teeth. He caught my eye in the mirror and did that little half nod kids do when they're clocking your mood without wanting to call it out.

We didn't speak. Nothing "happened." But both of us knew the weather. He knew whether the house felt light or heavy. I knew I was reading him reading me. That's when you realize the storm isn't just between two adults. It's in the air your kids are breathing.

A kid doesn't say, "Dad, your nervous system is loud." He just starts adapting. He talks a little less. He stays in his room a little more. He watches your face first and the TV second. And sometimes he tries to bring the pressure down for you through a joke, a random question, a little burst of energy. Kids will become tiny peacekeepers when they feel grown-up weather.

That's the part that still hits me when I look back. I thought I was protecting them by carrying it all. But they were living inside the carry. Every storm has a pressure drop—the moment the air shifts and you know something different is happening, even if you can't name it yet.

That week, I caught my first clean glimpse of what calm leadership could feel like. No speeches. No managing. No trying to control the weather inside the house. It didn't fix the storm. But it put a crack in the pattern. A seed planted for future Eric.

This Is Where the Noise Begins to Fade

If you zoomed out on my life during that season, you would still see the storm as my marriage began to dissolve. Like many things in my life, it happened slowly at first and then quickly at the end.

The divorce and all the proceedings around it were messy.

The kids, unfortunately, were caught in the middle and were triangulated often. Often it was a battle over which house the boys were supposed to be staying at. Or most commonly, money.

This was in prime 1.0 territory, so all the usual give-ins and overcorrecting were provided by me. The kids never got dragged into the proceedings, but the legal battles went on and on. My lawyer tried hard but was against a stacked deck.

My early thought process was simple: keep giving the same money I was giving before I left and that would show my good-faith intent. The standard "keep doing the right things and it will pay off in the long run" thinking.

I had the job at the time and the steady flow of money, but she had the kids. The statement at the beginning of the book is as true as it gets. The real thing a divorced dad worries about when the marriage ends is what will happen to his relationship with his kids. And by the time she made it to her third lawyer, I had been run ragged.

The esteemed Judge Caldwell awarded a monthly alimony-and-child-support payment higher than my monthly salary. When my lawyer protested, the judge said, "The two of you have overspent for too long. This award will control your spending."

Who knew I was in a budget seminar? I thought I was in a court of law. Long story short, we did not control our spending. The kids only got bigger, and the things they needed—like cars and insurance—only became more expensive.

I did what any broke divorced guy who'd lost the thirty-two-hundred-square-foot country-club house would do—I borrowed like mad on credit cards. Someday I will dig out of it. A buddy of mine once told me there is a reason that divorce is so expensive: "'Cause it's worth it."

New Season, New Me

As the divorce settled in and the years moved along, I slowly ramped up the quality of the places we lived. First an apartment in South Fork Village, then a townhouse on Rocky Falls Lane near the Publix. Then the first of the rental houses, one at Pam Drive (so many amazing memories) and today the new one off New Hope. Like a young couple in a starter home, me and the boys kept moving up, each time a little more comfortable with a little more space.

What I didn't realize then but do now, with the wisdom of hindsight, is that I was clearing out space internally as well. The hardened layers of bitterness from the last years of the marriage and the divorce had finally started to peel away.

As we spent more time living at Pam Drive, it began to show up in small, ordinary ways. Just a slight shift in orientation. I was starting to move through my own life with a little less tightening.

The boys seemed to sense it, matching a calmer pace in the quiet moments getting ready for school as we headed out on a dark morning. I could sit alone in my driveway, engine off, and admit something I hadn't let myself say yet: I was tired of carrying all of it.

Clarity arrives in small, repeatable moments—when your body begins to register another way to live. A quiet scene that stays with you. Men who don't rush. Quiet, peaceful mornings with the kids. None of that rewrote the history of my marriage overnight. None of it dissolved the storms.

Covid was a strange time for many people. I got laid off—that was the bad. But in the middle of it, I made a connection with a woman who shifted my viewpoint forever. It's hard to describe.

It was completely platonic, but she was my soulmate for a season of my life. People usually use that word for a lover, but she was something different.

It wasn't her brilliance or wit or charm but her simple ability to connect with me at a deep level. An emotional level. A level that adjusted in attunement without needing to ask for adjustment. We were always able to easily and truly connect. There was never a period of misaligned frequency—those first moments of a conversation when the person in your sphere isn't fully present yet. When that happens, you end up blocking the opportunity to connect, short-circuiting the conversation before you have a chance to establish that bond emotionally. That is what we will explore further in the book.

It took me some time to get there, and I didn't see it then, but what that season did was show me—slowly, insistently—that there was another version of me underneath all the scanning and managing and tensing. This is an important thing I learned. It wasn't a new me or a new you. A fresh lens, a different perspective, can bring out the you that was there all along.

A version of me that didn't need to grip so hard. A version that could hold Soft Eyes and a Strong Spine not just in rare, peaceful moments but in the living room, the kitchen, the hallway between my kids' rooms.

This is where the noise begins to fade. Not in a courtroom. Not in a fight. Not in a dramatic rupture. It loosens quietly. In ordinary rooms. In familiar spaces. In the nearly invisible shift from "I must control everything" to "maybe I can just be present."

NOTES FROM A DIVORCED DAD
What to Carry Forward

- Fog counts even when nobody's yelling
- Being the barometer is real labor, and it has a cost
- Kids feel weather before they understand words
- Overdrive can look like love and still create distance
- One calm moment isn't "nothing," it's proof your system can live another way

CHAPTER 3

THE DAY THE NOISE BROKE

The Game That Changed the Signal

There's a moment in every man's life when the noise he's been carrying for decades finally bumps into something that doesn't move. I didn't see it at the time because I wasn't aligned enough to realize it until twenty-five years later as I headed down this journey of mental clarity. But breadcrumbs were being dropped along the way like seeds of future growth being planted. The moments of enlightenment were there if I'd had the awareness to see.

Hidden under that old, foggy lens was the man I could be. The man I would become years later. The man I was meant to be—with a new way of seeing the world. Not a changed man or a new man, just me with a different perspective on my life. These are the moments I should have been paying attention to at the time, not the wrong jacket or the small stuff I thought mattered.

Sometimes it's earlier than we think—a quiet day that sets

the frequency, long before the MRI tube and the later chapters of your life. For me, it wasn't a crisis. It wasn't a court date. It wasn't a diagnosis. It was a baseball game. A single summer day in Atlanta with my dad.

If the early chapters were the wiring and the storm inside the house, this chapter is the wisdom of a new operating system. The day the noise in my life finally met a moment big enough, quiet enough, real enough that it had to sit down and catch its breath.

To get there, you need to know a little more about my father and about who I had become by the time I flew him down to Atlanta.

The Quiet Before the Noise Breaks

In your twenties and thirties, you assume life is supposed to be loud. Busy schedule loud. Travel itinerary loud. Two-career household loud. Car seats and baseball bags and mortgage payments loud.

You tell yourself this is just how it is. You work hard. You build a life. You say "yes" to everything that feels like "opportunity." You patch the holes as they show up. Looking back now, I can see how much of my early adulthood wasn't really me choosing a life—it was me repeating one.

That's why my dad matters here. Tom lived at a different frequency.

My father was the original "I'll swing by" salesman. He'd drive hours to a customer for a fifteen-minute conversation. He knew every back road, every shortcut. If you want a clean picture of Tom's steadiness, it wasn't in speeches. It was in the way he handled small heat quietly—the kind that leaves a burn mark under a sink and no drama in the air.

And then there was the night of the fish. I was in sixth grade, headed to a dusk game at the rec league field. My glove was by the door. Tom was one of the coaches, and he was always late. Maybe it was the traffic or maybe it was just him, but he never made it to things on time.

He came through the front door mid-sentence, jacket half on, shoes louder than they needed to be, and took the stairs two at a time. Then he stopped on the landing. Nose in the air. Something was different. Dinner was being cooked.

My mom had grown up in Winthrop, near the ocean, and they ate fish like some families ate roast chicken. To her it was normal to make fish for dinner. To Tom, it was an ambush. He let out that long Tom sound—not a word, more like a gravelly sigh that carried the whole day in it. "Ehhhh." Then, louder, like the hallway needed to hear it: "For Christ's sakes … fish?"

I don't remember the exact sentence she said. I remember the temperature. She'd been carrying the house all day, steady and unseen, and he walked in without reading the room. Something tipped. A moment later she came down the hall with the pan, calm in her body, like she was setting a tray on the table, and then—no ceremony—she let the fish go. It was quick. Hot. Done.

The fish caught him in the head and slid down onto the floor. Tom stood there for a second, eyes wide, like the room had shifted and he was still finding his footing. Then he did what he always did when the house got loud—he moved.

He didn't stop to clean anything up. He shook his head, knocked off what he could, and grabbed his big red team hat. There were still bits stuck in his hair when he shoved it on his head. He looked at me, pointed toward the door, and barked the line that meant the argument was over and the world was bigger than our kitchen:

"Ricky, grab your glove."

I grabbed it. We left. No lecture. No post-game analysis. Just motion.

At the field, Dan Miller took one look at him and started laughing. Tom didn't duck. He didn't shake it out. He leaned into it. "These bugs are gonna be loving me tonight," he said, like he'd planned it.

And sure enough, walking back to the cars after a win, the swarm made a little orbit around his hat. The other dads couldn't bust his chops fast enough. Tom just grinned and kept walking. We left that field with smiles from ear to ear.

Years later, when Tom was gone and the house got quiet in a different way, that story would still get told—because it had the whole man in it: take the hit, make it lighter, and keep going.

My childhood soundscape was the low murmur of WBZ or WEEI on the bedroom radio, the rustle of the *Globe* sports section, and the click of my dad's car keys hitting his dresser when he came home. I grew up watching a man build a life around motion.

So when I became an adult? I did the same. Flights, rental cars, customer visits, regional meetings, trade shows, plant tours. I'd joke to people that my job was really just as a professional line stander.

I could travel on autopilot. I knew where the shortest security lines were, which side of the terminal had better food, and how early you had to leave to hit a meeting across town without white-knuckling it.

On the outside, I looked like a man "on the rise." Solid job in technical sales. An emerging young family, a growing professional network, and a life with enough on paper that no one asked too many questions.

On the inside, I was running ahead of my own life. I didn't sit still. I converted anxiety into logistics. I treated being home like a layover between flights. It felt like responsibility. I'm providing. I'm building something. I'm doing what men are supposed to do. So keep doing it.

Before the awakening came the fog. Before the fog lifted came the hum. Before the hum became unbearable came the day that shaped everything. A day with my father. The last one that felt truly simple.

Tom, Baseball, and a Lifetime of Keeping Score

If you want to understand the day in Atlanta, you have to understand how baseball lived in my father's bones. Tom grew up when the Boston Braves were still the team, before they shipped off to Milwaukee and then Atlanta. He followed them religiously. City to city, roster to roster, decade to decade.

His Braves loyalty wasn't just about sports, though. His father—my Papa Stanley—was a huge Red Sox guy, the kind of old-school Boston man who wore a hat like it was part of the uniform of adulthood. He sold furniture, then moved up into industrial lubricants at MetroChem Industries. Straightlaced. Witty. The template.

Papa Stanley was so passionate, he listened to Sox games

with a little transistor radio and a white earpiece tucked into one ear whenever it was game day. Sometimes he'd hand me that earbud like it was a sacred object. It still had his wax on it. I didn't care. I shoved it in and listened anyway.

Tom picking the Braves, first Boston, then Milwaukee, then Atlanta, always felt like it had a second layer. Part genuine love for a local team. Part mischievous jab at the old man, like, "Yeah, I know you love the Sox. Watch me love somebody else, this other team in town."

That's how men in my family showed affection: through teams, teasing, and the quiet permission to belong. By the time I came along, the Braves were an Atlanta team and the Red Sox were our home team, but to Tom, the Braves never stopped being part of Boston.

He loved pitching. He loved clean defense. He loved games that were 2–1, where every pitch mattered.

He was the kind of guy who kept score with a pencil and a worn scorebook. I can vividly recall the tragic 1978 Red Sox loss. By then, after his father got sick, Tom had started calling himself a soft fan. As the final outs piled up, he stopped keeping score. That's when you knew it was over.

He'd sit in his leather recliner back then, WTBS on, and track every at-bat. By the time he was done, it looked like a line card they would show on TV. Filled out all the details. If I was downstairs watching, every once in a while, he'd pass me a piece of gum. Double Bubble.

That's what connection looked like at ten years old. Baseball on the TV or radio. Gum from your father. The sound of a pencil scratching out a box score. Years later, when I moved into a tiny Boston apartment during college, my life got wrapped even closer to the game.

It was the mid-80s. The Red Sox were in the middle of one of those seasons that makes the whole city feel like it's buzzing. My freshman year in college, 1986, was the season they lost to the Mets in seven games. If you know, you know. If you lived downtown that year, you really know.

I lived within walking distance of Fenway. You could feel the crowd from blocks away. You could hear the roar through brick. Money was tight. I was in college those years, but you didn't need to go to the game. You just charged into the streets after they won.

Those days with the Red Sox, I'd watch the games and stream out onto Landsdowne after each playoff and World Series game. The next day there was always a call from my dad to see if I'd been in Kenmore Square the night before. The answer was yes, of course, and the stories were nonstop.

We didn't have big heart-to-heart talks. We didn't "process." We watched. We listened. We kept score. Sports, and especially baseball, was the place where the noise of life faded into the background and something cleaner came through.

FIELD NOTES
Why Men Bond Side-by-Side

Men will drive eight hours to sit next to each other in a stadium seat.

Ask us to sit face-to-face and share our deepest

feelings for ninety minutes, and we'll tell you
we're busy.

It's not that we don't feel. It's that we were wired
to connect alongside something—work, a game,
a task, a project.

Side-by-side is not avoidance. It's how many men
feel safe enough to let their guard down.

The trick is learning how to bring that same
presence home.

The Track and the Language of Us

My dad had another world where he and I spoke fluent "Tom."
Not baseball. Horses.

There was a stretch where he'd use me as cover to go to the
track because my mom hated when he went. Even though she
knew anyway, it seemed I was part of the ruse. If I was there,
it looked less like gambling and more like "father-son time."
(Which, to be fair, it was.)

He liked the newer Plainville track because they didn't allow
smoking. He'd quit many years before, and he hated being around
smoke, so he'd walk in already half-relieved … and then complain anyway, because that was also part of the ritual.

He had rules like don't bet two Boston teams the same day
and weird little superstitions such as liking a grey horse when it

was live, not simulcast. Exclusively live. If he believed something, such as "don't wear heavy boots, they'll warp your brain," he held onto it tight.

One Breeders' Cup Day in the late '90s is burned into my head. We're standing under those big TVs. There are still live races going on, so he waddles over with that funny duck-walk he knew he had, the one he said got him in trouble in the Army, and he locks eyes on a grey horse.

He goes quiet, then lets out this slow, low whisper like he's talking to God through a straw, "Oooooh … lock up." Then he turns and booms it like an announcement to the entire state of Massachusetts:

"LOCK UP!"

"Ricky, Ricky … the six is grey."

Oh yeah, besides his quirky sayings, he loved numbers. His numbers were two and six and if he needed a third: one, two, six. Anytime he needed a number, they were there at the ready. So seeing a grey six was like a sign from above. We bet and headed over to the TVs, which, if you're paying attention, was another Tom-ism. It is always better luck to watch on the TVs than the actual race, even if you are there.

Turns out that he bet too much on the six, along with his usual flurry of exacta and trifecta boxes and other exotics that only he and some other regulars knew how to bet. The ol' six may still have been running, but I had played my numbers, two and five, my birthday, and boxed a two-five exacta along with his ill-fated six.

There was a point in the race when we were under the TVs, and he started to flip through his stack of tickets as if they might change. They did not. He looked over and I just casually showed him my two-five ticket. Tom did not have good eyesight, but he could see a betting slip from across a room.

Suddenly his mood changed as it started to look good. All of a sudden he started to do that ramp-up again, the hush-toned "oooooh, lock up," then another ... and then one of those full-volume Tom declarations as the horses came down the stretch.

Another guy tried to tell him one of my horses got nicked, but he wasn't having any of that noise. It came home and when it hit, he was ecstatic, as if it was his ticket. Not because he won.

Because I won.

It was always about if I won with Tom. And that's the part people miss about men like my dad. The language and the noise and the superstition ... underneath it was devotion. It was his unflinching loyalty, of him defending me to a stranger over a photo finish. It was him rooting for his kid like it was his honor.

His language was loud. The love underneath it was louder. That's why the day in Atlanta matters. Because it's the same frequency, the same father-son bond, just in a quieter room.

The Day I Flew My Father Down

Fast-forward a handful of years and I'm working a job that coincidently has me in Atlanta on occasion for training. The Braves are in one of their great runs during those pitching years where it felt like every night another ace was on the mound. Interleague play is still a new trick MLB is rolling out.

They announced the schedule in the offseason, and for the first time American League and National League teams would finally cross over in real, meaningful games. You had Yankees and Mets along with some other flashy matchups. But there was one that lit up every circuit in my father's chest.

Red Sox vs. Braves

The team of my Boston childhood versus the team he'd followed all the way to Atlanta. I looked at that schedule and had one clean, simple thought. *I'm flying my dad down.* Not to impress him. Not to prove I'd "made it." Not to repair anything. Just to give him something he'd quietly earned. A day where he didn't have to carry anything.

The labor on my side was just some time and late nights on the phone with airlines, figuring out mileage bookings. Shifting my work travel so I was actually in town that week. Arranging my training and a couple of meetings so I could protect a full day for the game. Lining up a hotel, a rental car, the logistics my wiring loves.

Tickets to the game were the bigger mission. This was before StubHub made it feel like tickets were a commodity. Hot games took effort, calls, favors, timing, luck. And when I finally had two good seats and an itinerary that worked, I felt that specific kind of relief men don't talk about. Not excitement … relief. Like I had successfully protected a small piece of joy in a world that usually steals those pieces if you don't guard them.

When I picked Dad up at the hotel and we drove toward Turner Field, we talked about normal things. A little about my new job, the Bruins, and anything that happened to scroll across his mind. Talking was always his favorite thing to do.

Every few minutes, he'd slip something in like, "Boy, I still can't believe we are going to see the Sox and the Braves."

Walking into the Quiet

Some places are built for noise. Stadium concourses are one of them. You've got the echo of footsteps on concrete, vendors shouting about hot dogs and peanuts, the scent of beer and grilled onions, crowd noise rolling in waves from the seating bowl.

We had someone take a picture of us on the concourse. We bought ballpark food. I remember watching my dad watch the park. You could tell he was mentally mapping it out—taking in the sightlines, the outfield grass, the way the seating arched around home plate.

There's a specific way a lifelong baseball guy looks at a stadium: half fan, half architect. We found our seats—good ones, better than he expected—and sat down.

It should have been chaos. But that day walking into Turner Field with my father, something felt different. I wasn't rushing. I wasn't checking my watch. I wasn't running mental simulations about the rest of my schedule.

What I really wanted then was someone to quietly mark the moment. To say, without making a thing of it, that these were the good times—and that they weren't accidental. That connection can and will happen, not just because of the setting or a big event like this, but because of the emotional availability you bring with you.

That game was one of the first times in my adult life my nervous system wasn't three steps ahead. We stopped and looked around. We got there a little early to check out the Braves museum. They had plenty of old-school Boston Braves artifacts.

I don't remember every pitch of the game. I remember this: We had nothing to solve. Nothing to negotiate. No old disagreements floating in the air. We were just there. Two men at a ball game. No roles. No emotional weather blowing through the moment. Just presence.

The Scorebook, the Soda Fountain, and the Feeling of Enough

Of course he kept score. He bought a scorecard and a pencil, settled in, and started filling in lineups. At some point, the card ended up balanced across both our knees. I'd call out a number, some baseball jargon like that was a six–three (shortstop to first base ground out), and he'd mark the play.

In between innings, we talked. Not about "how are we really doing?" Not about family tension. Not about money or stress or anything heavy. We talked about whether the manager should've hit-and-run, how good the Braves' pitching really was. Old stories about the Boston Braves, as if they might run out of the dugout any minute.

And then there were the little moments that don't make the highlight reel but somehow become the whole memory. There was some cheesy in-between-innings promotion, pick which song is better, something like that. He nudges me: "Boy, boy ... which one?" I half-heartedly shrug and say the first thing that comes to mind: "I dunno ... Smash Mouth, 'All Star.'"

It was right. You would've thought I'd cured cancer. "Ricky, how did you know that?" We laughed like idiots, and for a second

I was ten again, and he was just my dad, and none of the future heaviness had arrived yet. The Braves would rally late to win with six runs in the ninth. The place was electric but there was no bragging that his team won or that this was "the year." It seemed on that day he didn't even notice the score. It was just about the day at the ballpark.

After the game, we didn't go to the famous Atlanta place everybody talks about, *The Varsity*. Neither of us felt like standing in a line that wrapped around the block. So we went to a sub shop near Turner Field, medium busy, still buzzing with fans.

We ordered, grabbed cups, and slid into that crowded soda fountain area where everyone's doing the polite dance of elbows and ice. Dad got cut off by a guy who didn't see him. Without thinking, I reached past, grabbed his cup, and filled it for him. He looked at me and gave me that Tommy ear-to-ear smile—big pumpkin head, proud eyes, the kind of grin that says a whole paragraph without using a single word.

That's the version of "enough" I'm talking about in this chapter. Not the big dramatic kind. The quiet kind that shows up when a man is seen, helped, included, and doesn't have to ask. The noise in my life didn't disappear that day. The bills, the marriage, the career pressure, they were all still waiting back home.

But for those hours, something deeper than noise settled in. There was a moment that I can still see now where I looked over and saw my father not as "Dad" or "provider" or "the guy who worked until the very end, selling paper products," but as a man who had the ability to ignore life's weight and set it all down in a plastic stadium seat to watch a game with his son.

FIELD NOTES

When Your Nervous System Takes a Day Off

Most men don't know they're tightened until the moment they aren't.

Signs your nervous system briefly took the day off:

- You don't care what time it is
- You're not rehearsing conversations in your head
- You're not tracking anyone's micro-moods
- You forget your phone for half an inning

That feeling? That's your baseline. Not the tension you've normalized.

The work of this whole book is learning how to live more days from that baseline—without needing a baseball game to get you there.

The Moment the Noise Finally Met Its Match.

So why does this day matter so much? Because for the first time in my adult life, I got a glimpse of what it could look like if I stopped running ahead of my own story. I wasn't using the game to prove anything. There was no performative need being fulfilled.

It was simple, just a way to be honest and pure and enjoy being who you are. Beyond just enjoying life. Comfortable with yourself. I wasn't using the trip to show my father I'd "made it." I wasn't over-functioning, trying to orchestrate every detail of his experience. I flew him down. I picked him up. And then I let that day be what it was.

We walked at the same pace. That seems small, but when you've spent your life three steps ahead emotionally, physically, mentally, that tiny alignment is massive.

On some level I couldn't articulate then, my nervous system got a new data point. You can live a whole day without tensing. You can be a good son and a good man without overperforming. It took twenty-five years to replace the foggy lens I had with a clean, fresh 2.0 lens, but this was the seed being planted.

You can let joy be simple. That Braves game didn't fix my patterns. It wouldn't heal my marriage. It didn't erase the overdrive that still ran my life. But it did something almost as important. It showed me that quiet was possible.

That there was a way of being with another person, especially someone as central as a parent, where the noise finally sat down. Years later, when the MRI tube and the escalators and the bridges would finally force me to stop running, this day is one of the anchors I'd reach back for.

"You've felt this before," my body would say. "You've walked like this before. You've breathed like this before." The day with my dad in Atlanta became proof that the version of me I was trying to find—the calm, soft-eyed, strong-spined man—wasn't a fantasy. He'd already shown up once.

The Call

My dad died in late 2000, two years after that Braves game. I can write that sentence clean on a page. Living it didn't come clean. It was an odd time of the year, that lull between Christmas and New Years. It was a soft workweek, but I was in the home office.

The phone rang and I looked down at the old fashioned caller ID box, and it was my mom. The kind of caller ID that for some reason changes the air in the room before you even answer.

When I picked up, the voice on the other end didn't have much breath for warm-up. No runway. Just the words "Dad's had an accident."

There are moments your brain doesn't accept at the speed your ears do. My hearing worked fine. At the hospital, my body didn't. It went cold and heavy at the same time. Like the floor got a little farther away.

I remember looking at whatever was in front of me and seeing right through the walls, carpets. It was all translucent. This is where the noise breaks for real. Up until then, the noise in my life had been mostly self-made: my pace, my proving, my clenching. After that call, the noise got teeth. Grief doesn't just hurt. It signs contracts inside you.

"Never again on my watch," my body wrote. "Don't get caught sleeping. Don't get caught soft. Don't let the people you love walk out of the room without you being ready."

And here's the strange part: In the middle of that new hardness, a small, ridiculous memory floated up—Tom, stunned in the hallway, fish in his hair, hat on crooked like a joke he wouldn't let die.

"Ricky, grab your glove."

When I was ten, that line meant: We're leaving the noise and going to the field. After the call, there was no glove to grab. No field to run to. Just a phone in my hand and a new weight in my chest.

That's what death did to my frequency. It took a man who had learned—just once—how to walk at the same pace as someone he loved … and it dared him to stay that soft without folding.

NOTES FROM A DIVORCED DAD
What to Carry Forward

- Sudden loss can harden existing wiring; it doesn't need permission
- "Never again on my watch" is a contract the body signs in grief
- Carrying everything can feel noble and still be unsustainable
- You can't white-knuckle randomness, heartbreak, or life
- The crack starts when you admit: Tightness is not protection

PART II

THE
AWAKENING

Awakening sounds spiritual. It is actually more mechanical. It's the moment you realize the system you've been running—your habits, your tone, your default reactions—has stopped producing the life you say you want.

This part is about the first cracks. The first honest looks. The scenes where you finally feel the cost of doing it the way you've always done it. Not just the cost to you—your stress, your sleep, your health—but the cost to the people living near your weather.

For me it was a series of deaths that forced me to get a glimpse of the person I could be. The person I was meant to be. Paul in 2025, Mark in 2024, and Tom back in 2000. The death of Paul was the start of my introspective journey.

The next chapters will provide you with recognition. And recognition is power. Because the minute you can name what's happening inside you—speeding up, ratcheting down, reaching for control—you create a gap. Naming it frames it and changes perspective.

This part is where the room begins to change. Not because everyone else suddenly behaves. Because you start catching the signal before you transmit the noise.

THE LONG ROAD BACK

Back to Center

At some point in a man's life, the mirror stops reflecting surface-level improvements and starts showing the things he doesn't want to admit. The lens you have been viewing the world with is foggy. You can try and clean the lens like you have been doing, but it needs a full replacement. These are the deeper reflections. The ones that hurt in strange, quiet places. The ones that don't go away when you turn off the bathroom light.

We've swerved around this topic. But now we meet it head-on. My daughter's estrangement. It's a strong word. Not melodramatic, not exaggerated, just accurate.

Around the same time back in 2017, when my own situation began to take shape, I watched something similar happen in my extended family: Two adults who were part of a close, tight orbit—one day, suddenly, weren't.

I'm not telling that story here. It isn't mine to tell. But seeing it up close taught me one simple thing: Estrangement is more common than people think, even in families that look sturdy from the outside.

It didn't make my situation easier. It didn't soften the grief. But it did at times pull me out of the lonely corner where your mind wants to hide when you feel like you're the only parent on earth living inside this kind of silence.

My daughter and I haven't seen each other since early 2017 when I left the house before the divorce was finalized in 2018. Since then, we've had the occasional transactional texts, mostly logistics. Never a real conversation. Never a phone call. Never the easy, familiar back-and-forth we used to have.

In the early years, I tried. I sent cards. Birthday messages. Holiday notes. "I love you, I'm here when you're ready." But that day never came.

I kept up with her life the way distant fathers do—through my youngest son Connor, through small updates that floated back to me, through the quiet knowledge that she and her brother maintained a growing relationship.

Anna has always been extraordinary. None of that changed after the divorce. She kept rising. Graduated from the University of Virginia. Went on to earn her master's degree.

Anna's wins are hers. Mine is the privilege of noticing them quietly, respectfully, without grabbing at the story. When she graduated from UVA, I wasn't there. Not by choice. I simply wasn't part of that orbit anymore.

So I did the only thing that felt clean: I sent a small, quiet gift. Nothing performative. Nothing manipulative. Just a simple, understated acknowledgment.

One short note basically saying, "I'm proud of you. I'm still cheering for you from where I am." She replied with a polite thank-you. Not warm, not cold. Just steady. It was the kind of exchange you have with someone you love deeply but don't have access to. And I took it for what it was. Proof she was still out there, still rising, still moving forward.

And proof that, sometimes, loving your child means admiring their life from the distance they choose. Over time, your heart starts doing a strange, defensive thing. It hardens around the truth. *Her life is complete without me in it.* And then, in the same breath, it softens around the other truth. *I still want every good thing for her regardless.*

For dads in this situation—and there are far more of us than people admit—you know the math: No amount of guilt, long messages, apologies, or even money as emotional currency can pull a grown child toward you unless that child wants to take the step.

Nothing moves until they want to move. But this is not a grief chapter. Not a pity chapter. Not even a tragedy. It's a chapter about the return—subtle, slow, and almost invisible—and the girl who made me proud before any of the silence began. To understand the road back, you must first understand the light we had before the long winter.

FIELD NOTES
Pride Without Claim

There's a thin line here, and dads cross it without realizing.

> Pride says: "I see you. I'm happy for you. I'm grateful I got to witness you becoming you."
> Claim says: "Look what I made."

Before the Distance Set in—"She Can Skate"

The truth is, Anna was extraordinary from the beginning. Not in a parent-inflated way. In the observable, quiet, "Oh wow, this kid has something" way.

It was Massachusetts, early 2005. A cold snap froze the drainage pond across from Town Spa Pizza in Stoughton. The exact kind of place that only people from that area understand. It's not a postcard pond. It's not picturesque. It's a drainage pond across from a pizza place and some woods.

But that winter? It froze just like in those old New England winters from the '70s and early '80s. I told Anna stories from my childhood—playing pond hockey with duct-taped gloves and homemade nets, skating until dark with Marty and the Hickey brothers after school.

Anna listened with that wide-eyed childhood focus that's half belief, half dare. I got her real hockey skates and a stick. She tried them on. Most kids collapse inward at the ankles, clinging to furniture the way a baby deer tests its legs.

Anna walked around the living room like she'd been born in the Montreal Canadiens locker room. It reminded me of a moment earlier that summer. She was wearing a swim diaper on her head, naturally, while performing what she considered a dance in the middle of the living room.

We were supposed to leave for Mark's pool. I said, "Hey, Ann, can we put the swim diaper on so we can go?" She didn't miss a beat. "When I am finished dancing." That was Anna. Always on her own internal timeline. Always knowing what needed to be done, but in the order she preferred.

Back to the pond. Across from Town Spa, there were little pockets of people out there—kids wobbling in clumps, a couple dads doing the slow-lap thing, and a few different size groups playing pond hockey.

No rentals. No staff. Just New England rules: Bring your stuff, tie your skates wherever you can find a rock, and try not to fall in front of your kid. I remember buckling her skates and thinking: *Okay, here comes the part where she grabs my hand and we shuffle along.*

She didn't wait. She pushed off. And she could skate. Not "cute kid for ten seconds" skate. Real skate. The kind where she glides into her balance instead of searching for it.

I did my one good hockey move: three hard strides, a tight turn to the right. Never could go left, me and Zoolander. A little spray-stop mostly for my own ego as I came up closer to her, and she just smiled like, Yeah, okay, Dad. Now watch this.

She drifted right toward the other kids, like she belonged there. Like the ice was an old friend. That moment landed in my chest as simple math. She's going to be fine.

We skated a bunch of times that winter. The twins were young, just past one, but we bundled them up and took 'em out a couple times. And looking back, those trips to the pond were the earliest hints of her independence, the quiet kind that doesn't announce itself but defines a person anyway.

The Walk-Off Homer

A few years later, after we moved to the Charlotte area, it was time for softball. Machine pitch. Anna at the plate. Game tied. Late inning. Kids buzzing. I'm coaching and trying not to get too excited.

Anna digs in. Machine fires. She swings. Crack. Ball sails so clean it smacks the school wall and ricochets. It was over the moment she hit it. Barrel meets ball, clean with that unmistakable composite bat crunch.

Then a thunk off the school wall that made every parent's head snap at the same time. For a second there's silence like the whole field has to confirm what just happened, and then the place erupts. A walk-off, in the Little League sense. She is running the bases one hundred miles an hour as the little girls helplessly run after the ball miles away.

The team waits for her at home plate, ready to erupt like she's Big Papi crossing home at Fenway. I'm standing in front of the dugout area, jumping up and down with them.

She rounds third, running hard with this tiny grin—not a showy one, just a "yeah, I did that" grin—and touches home. It wasn't the homer. It was the composure. It was the look of a kid who trusts herself.

The Summer She Swam with a Cast

Then came the broken leg. Skateboard accident. Her first day trying it. A bad break in every sense of the word. She had been swimming competitively yearlong with Ethan. They had been doing it for years at this point and took it seriously. Most kids would've spent the summer benched. Anna swam. Every practice. Every meet.

She wore this inflatable cast protector that looked like a cross between medical gear and a pool toy. Pump it up, seal it, pray it holds—because if it leaked, it wasn't just annoying. It was a hard stop.

It tore constantly. We needed to keep buying replacements. She didn't care. She was in the water. She even won some heats. Replace, adjust, keep going. She wasn't chasing records that summer. She was chasing participation.

That season she still found a way to stay in the water. Practice. Meets. The whole loop. And the part that still gets me is how undramatic she was about it. No speeches. No self-pity. Just: "Okay. When do we leave?"

One of my favorite stories of Anna comes from this time. I was still working with my friend Wade, one of the steadiest, most grounded men on earth. We traveled together often, but when we were in the office, we'd also usually grab lunch with some others and talk about our kids.

Wade asked, "How's Anna doing with that cast?" I lit up. Told him how she'd competed all summer, blow-up protector and all, and how she even won a couple of her heats with that big plastic boot on her leg.

Wade paused, smirked, and said in his soft Southern drawl, "Ha … I'd hate to be one of the kids who finished behind her." I nearly lost it laughing. Still smile now writing that.

That's the thing about Anna. She didn't sit out life because it was inconvenient. She swam through obstacles, literally.

The County Championship Year

Through middle school, her world also included basketball. Seventh grade. Then eighth. She wasn't the stat-sheet star. She was the backbone: rebounding, defense, hustle, the glue player every coach dreams about.

The eighth-grade team made a run all the way to the county championship. There is a great photo of her in front of the school sign after they won the championship, uniform on, smiling in that quiet, proud way. I can recall "senior night," eighth-grade edition. They called her name. I stood next to her.

We walked across the gym floor together, applause echoing off the walls. I didn't know it then, but it would be our last completely uncomplicated moment. I didn't know our world would fracture within a year. I didn't know the distance was coming. I just knew I was proud.

How Distance Really Happens

Estrangement rarely arrives with one dramatic moment. It's almost never a blowout fight, a slammed door, or a single catastrophic event. It's more like erosion. Slow, quiet, cumulative.

Freshman year arrives. My ex and I split up. Schedules shift. Two households develop different emotional climates. Stories get told and retold in rooms you're not in. Kids learn who's "easier," who's "safer," who's "present by default," and who requires emotional calibration to be around.

And while it's tempting to blame someone or something, the truth is simpler and harder. Distance forms in the emotional cracks none of us notice when we're stressed, tired, or hurting. It was a long-forming wound like a callous.

It was gradual. I would try to reach out or send a note, but it was a confusing time for a young teenager.

My old lens added to the stress by trying to correct. All good intentions, all with love in my heart. A few life coaches and therapists to try and find a way to connect. What I truly did not understand at the time was that my misguided alignment of our emotional frequencies blocked any possible connection from taking place. Time went on and months turned to years.

The contact became purely transactional. The occasional invitation went unanswered. Cards or money went unacknowledged. Just … quiet. The quiet that accumulates when a child's emotional survival instinct leans them toward one orbit over another.

And I was in the outer orbit. Connor became the bridge. One of the few comforting constants in those years was Connor's relationship with her. He'd give me updates. Nothing intrusive, nothing gossipy. Just the little things siblings share naturally. She's loving her classes, she's getting her masters, she's coming home this weekend.

It meant everything to know she still had solid family around her even if that family wasn't me at the moment. If you're a dad reading this in a similar situation, that's a key truth. Your kid being okay is always more important than your kid being in contact with you.

FIELD NOTES
What Not to Do When
Your Estranged Child Texts Back

Do Not:

- Send paragraphs apologize for nine years in one message
- Say "this means so much to me"
- Ask if you're "okay now"
- Treat one message like a reconciliation

Do:

- Match their pace
- Stay warm but brief
- Let the thread end naturally
- Let the next thread begin when they initiate it
- Keep becoming a man worth reconnecting with

A child will not reenter a relationship if doing
so feels like stepping into a vortex of their
parent's need.
Closeness cannot be forced.
But safety can be offered.

The Parallel Road to Tom

Let me tell you something I didn't understand until I was
writing this book. My possible road back to Anna has a shadow

twin—my relationship with my father, Tom. Not in a dramatic, psychological-wound way. In a surprisingly tender, circular way.

Years later, I see the symmetry. My last simple, pure moment with Tom was at Turner Field. My last simple, pure moment with Anna was that middle school senior night.

Both moments were ordinary. Both became mythic in hindsight. Both live in my chest like gentle weights I am able to now carry with gratitude, not grief. And the connection between the two surprised me. The quiet way Tom showed up in that moment is the quiet way I want to show up for Anna now.

Not pushing. Not forcing. Not grabbing at closeness. Just standing where she can see me. Steady. Warm. Findable. Not tightened. Not hurting out loud. Not requesting too much emotional bandwidth. Just a father, available at the right frequency.

The Long Silence

Here is where we calibrate tone carefully. Because reality is what the relationship has quietly evolved to today. It wasn't dramatic how we got here. It wasn't filled with fights or ugly scenes. It was just a slow drift.

The kind that happens when a daughter grows up in an emotional climate where a father is trying too hard or not hard enough. At the times when two nervous systems fall out of sync, and the noise of divorce rearranges a family in ways no one planned. It was the absence of moments, not the presence of conflict, that created the long silence.

I'd send occasional holiday texts. Short birthday lines. Every now and then, a simple "I love you, I'm here when you're ready." Not fishing lines. Not guilt bombs. Just threads.

Most of the time, silence came back. Silence can feel like a verdict if you let it. But over the time of my own awakening, it began to feel like the reality of something as present as the weather instead. Not personal. Not permanent. Just the atmospheric reality between us.

Being honest and naming it helps frame it. Once you see it, you can't unsee it. Viewing it with a grounded Soft Eyes, Strong Spine viewpoint allows a sense of understanding.

There's a certain dignity in accepting what is without rewriting it into something dramatic or self-punishing. That's when I started to grow up as a father. Not in the biological sense. In the emotional one.

The Text That Didn't Look Like a Breakthrough

Nine years of distance. One logistical message. That's how the thaw began. I reached out to tell Anna it was time for her to take over her phone plan. She had graduated and found a new job, so the timing felt right at that point in our relationship.

Eric 1.0 would've packed that text with subtext, reassurance, apology, emotional cushioning, fear of being misinterpreted, a quiet plea for closeness. But at that season in my life, I had already begun turning inward—early morning drives alone, where the thinking was clear and unhurried.

My nervous system had changed. My frequency had recalibrated. I had started this transformation I am referring to as moving from 1.0 to 2.0. From a tightened hyper-vigilant, over-correcting father to a calm easy-to-breathe-around father.

The text was simple. Clean. Clarified. Here's the date. Here's what you'll need. Let me know if you have questions. No emotional pressure. No fishing line cast into her silence.

This is crucial. Children, even adult children, can feel the emotional weather behind your words. This may be an optimistic slant, looking for the smallest gleam of light. But when you have transformed as I have, there is a shift people around you notice.

So when the text came back, it wasn't just the timing or the tone. It wasn't the same—transactional. She felt the shift instantly. For the first time in nearly a decade, she replied warmly.

Not a paragraph. Not a confession of missing me. Just a natural, easy, unforced reply. The miracle wasn't in what she said. The miracle was in what she didn't say. She didn't tighten. She didn't pull back. She didn't freeze.

It was the first half-inch of relaxation, the same tiny drop in her shoulders I used to see when I'd tuck her in as a little girl. And in reconnection work, a half-inch is everything.

The Slow Thaw

Real reconnection is a slow process. There's no airport run, no teary doorstep reunion in the rain, no orchestral swell. It arrives like a shift in weather. Quietly, gradually, then all at once you notice you aren't bundled up anymore.

After the phone-plan moment, the space between me and Anna didn't transform overnight. There was no "now we're fixed" moment. Just a slight warming of tone.

A message answered without hesitation. A text sent without tension. A silence that didn't feel loaded. A reply that didn't feel obligatory. A closeness that didn't register as threat.

The year moved along, and I made a hardened decision to

not send a birthday gift. It was more reflexive and not something that felt right at the time. I would like to think it was a glitch or slight setback in the new operating system. There are many dynamics at play with gift giving, but the short analysis is it wasn't the right move. Using money as emotional currency one way or the other is the worst thing you can do with your kids, or anyone.

When Christmas approached I decided to send a Venmo with a little cash and a short text. I sent it because I love her and I wanted her to have something extra at Christmas. Simple. No reason to get into deep tradeoffs and "what about my feelings" or how it will be interpreted. Make a decision that you feel right about at the time and move forward. Life keeps moving on.

I was delighted to get a short but warm reply not long after I sent the money. It was brief. We don't want to get too far out over our skis but, similar to the earlier text, there was a new sense of warmth and maybe even a modicum of connection.

This is what it can look like. A daughter answering a message in hours instead of months. A father not over-analyzing what every emoji means. A shared tone that feels natural, not cautious. A thread that ends gently, not abruptly. A thread that begins again later, on her terms, not mine.

If you are a father in this situation, the hardest thing is not holding hope. The hardest thing is not clutching hope too hard. Because clinging is the enemy. Grasping becomes emotional static. White-knuckling is a frequency kids back away from.

Warmth is invitation. Calm is invitation. Steadiness is invitation. Forcing is noise. When the noise stops, the thaw begins. When your emotional baggage blocks the opportunity for connection, you can never repair.

The Work of Not Rushing the Moment

There is a moment in every estranged parent's journey where you feel the urge to sprint. To accelerate the closeness. To capitalize on the momentum. To make up for all the years in a single conversation.

Resist that urge. 2.0 doesn't force the pace. 2.0 doesn't overreach. 2.0 doesn't narrate the thaw as proof of redemption. 2.0 stays grounded in his life, in his presence, in his untightened posture.

When Anna sent those two warmer replies in the spring and then again during the holidays, old me would've sent a cascade of follow-ups. "It's so good to hear from you." "I've missed you so much." "We should talk soon." "Are you open to getting together?"

None of these are wrong. They're just heavy. They're hooks disguised as tenderness that are emotional ransom. This time, I did something completely new. I answered what she actually said. And then I stopped talking.

That's when I realized a key truth of all reconnection work. Sometimes the most loving thing a father can do is not speak.

FIELD NOTES
The Frequency Check

Is your emotional signal tuned, scrambled,
or silently draining the room? Every man
broadcasts a frequency. Not through words.
Through presence.

Your kids hear it. Your partner feels it. Your body pays for it.

This check takes less than a minute and tells the truth faster than any journaling app ever will.

Step 1: The Internal Signal

Ask yourself, what's the real frequency I'm broadcasting right now?

Choose one:

- Steady: calm enough to be trusted
- Hot: anxious, over-explaining, managing every molecule in the room
- Cold: withdrawn, quiet but not peaceful
- Split: acting one way, feeling another
- Static: exhausted, reactive, unpredictable

Whatever word you circle, that's the frequency your kids have already felt today.

Step 2: The External Impact

Now ask, how does my frequency shape the room I'm walking into?

- Do people soften around me? Or tighten?
- Do conversations relax? Or do people start editing themselves?
- Do my kids lean toward me? Or hover near the doorway?

Frequency is not about tone. It's about safety.

Step 3: The Correction

You don't fix frequency by force. You fix it by one small recalibration.

- One slower breath, one unclenched jaw
- One pause before responding, one honest answer instead of a polished one
- One moment of choosing presence over performance

This is tuning, not transforming. The smallest adjustment changes the whole field.

Step 4: The Exit Question

Finish with the only question that matters:

"Would I want my son or daughter to inherit this frequency?"

If the answer is no, you already know the adjustment you need to make.

If the answer is yes, you're already becoming the man you once needed.

The Road Back

This is the part where a lesser book would promise a perfect ending. No. The road back is not neat. It's not linear. You don't keep on leveling up to reach the summit and get that big hug. It's a practice. Its micro-fixes that add up to large gains. A posture. A frequency. A way of showing up that doesn't demand an outcome.

Since the phone-plan moment and Christmas text, I have noticed a shift in tone from the comments I get from her brothers. I do sit and think at times what a reach out from her might read like. But in those moments, I don't go sprinting into fantasies of reconciliation. I don't think about reaching out for a connection. I don't reach emotionally. I savor what is here, not what is missing.

Because here's the truth about fatherhood no one says: Even without access, a father can still be a father. Even without contact, a father can still hold love. Even without a seat in the front row, a father can still stand steady.

Anna returning even slightly is not the result of a strategy. It's the result of a climate. My climate shifted, and in kind her climate toward me shifted. And in that shift, the distance warmed by a few degrees. That's the road back. Not a reunion but a redirection. A path quietly reappearing between two people who once shared a whole universe.

NOTES FROM A DIVORCED DAD
What to Carry Forward

- Reconnection isn't a sprint, it's a pace of safety
- Showing up calmly matters more than showing up loudly
- Pressure can interrupt progress even when your intentions are good
- Trust returns in small, voluntary steps
- Your job is steadiness, not persuasion

HOW I RUINED A GOOD DRIVER

The Cost of the Wrong Frequency

Teaching your kid how to drive doesn't arrive with the drama it deserves. There's no ceremony. No applause. No "Congratulations, you've entered a new phase of terror." It shows up like most big fatherhood milestones do, disguised as paperwork and logistics. A learner's permit. A little checklist. A text from a kid that says "hey, Dad, can we go drive later?"

You walk out to the driveway with your kid, hand over the keys, and you clench up in a way your mouth doesn't have words for yet. This isn't a bike anymore.

When they were little, you ran alongside them with one hand on the seat, yelling, "Pedal, pedal, pedal," pretending you weren't scared. If they fell, it was blood and gravel and maybe a couple stitches if the pavement felt spicy that day. You cleaned it up. You told the story later. It turned into a memory.

A car is different. A car has mass. Momentum. Speed. A

car turns mistakes into invoices. A car changes insurance rates, schedules, and your kid's sense of themselves. A car is the first real "I can go" that doesn't require you to be in the same room.

For a dad with a 1.0 lens, teaching a kid to drive let the overthinking, overanalyzing, over-teaching version of me take the wheel. Every alarm in my nervous system went off at once. Eric 1.0 showed up strong there. It's also where I made one of the cleanest mistakes of my life—not because I didn't care, but because I cared too tightly.

The Fog I Didn't Know I Was In

Looking back, I can see I was already tired by the time Owen started driving. Not "worked a long week" tired. I mean the kind of tired that makes your nervous system jumpy even on good days. The divorce fog was still hanging around, that low-grade hum of fear under your skin when you're convinced you're one bad moment away from messing something up with your kids.

Every milestone carries extra weight. Every interaction feels like evidence. You start believing that if you don't manage things perfectly, something important will slip through your fingers. You don't notice it as a thought. You notice it as posture. As tone. As how quickly you give advice, how quickly you rush to "help," how quickly you try to get control of the moment.

Driving felt like one of those moments. Because driving isn't just driving. It's independence.

How I Ended Up in the Passenger Seat (Poor Owen)

When Anna reached driving age, she was already living full-time with her mom. We didn't spend time in the car together. Ethan went through driver's ed mostly with his mom too. We did some driving, but by the time we were together in the car, he was already a nicely molded lump of clay. He was calm. He listened. He didn't need constant narration from me.

Owen was different. Maybe it was schedules. Maybe it was the amount of time he spent at my house compared to Ethan at that phase. Either way, I became Owen's driving coach. Poor Owen.

He didn't know it at the time, but my foggy lens jammed his driving radar. This wasn't because he lacked ability. Owen had every trait a good driver needs: athletic, quick reflexes, great eyesight (no glasses), super aware, a generally confident young man.

He wasn't a reckless kid. He wasn't out there doing *Fast & Furious* stunts. He was capable. And that's what makes this story painful: I didn't need to grip that hard. I just couldn't stop myself yet.

Eric 1.0 Takes the Wheel

The old wiring used to mistake vigilance for leadership. So I turned every drive into a rolling seminar, a driver's education video delivered at thirty-five miles per hour. Check your mirrors. Always read what the other drivers are doing. Keep an eye out for everything.

Don't hug the line too close. Stay calm. Stay confident. I actually told him stay calm and confident like he had any chance with me sitting next to him vibrating like a smoke alarm.

And here's the thing: My advice wasn't technically wrong. That's the sneaky part. Plenty of it was good driving instruction. Mirror checks matter. Reading traffic matters. Awareness matters.

But frequency matters more than content. In my 1.0 state, even correct advice had a grabby feeling under it. Like I was trying to regulate my panic by regulating his driving. It was interference dressed up as instruction.

FIELD NOTES
The Frequency Check (in a Car)

Soft Eyes = See without tensing.
Strong Spine = Stay steady without coiling.

If you can do it in the passenger seat, you can do it anywhere. Ask yourself, mid-drive:
Am I teaching … or regulating?
Is my voice calm … or loaded?
Is my face relaxed … or scanning?
Am I commenting to help him … or commenting to help me?

Kids don't need perfect dads. They need adjustable ones.

The "Hours Logged" Season

With a learner's permit, you have to log a certain number of hours. Which means you don't just do one Saturday lesson and call it a day. You're in the car together a lot.

So we drove. Over and over. We'd head out toward Crowders

Mountain because we liked it out that way—pretty area, horse farms, long acreage, a little space to breathe. It's where we'd fish sometimes. It's where I once hiked to the top with Owen and Connor on a sunny afternoon.

Crowders is also where you can get lulled into thinking the roads will behave. They don't. And those drives became a pattern: Owen would settle in, hands steady, shoulders relaxed … and my mouth would start. I could feel the moment the air tightened.

Not in a dramatic way. Just a small shift—his grip a little firmer, his eyes flicking more often to the mirrors, his breathing getting shallower. He'd start checking my face without meaning to, like he was trying to read whether he was doing it "right."

That last part is the tell. Kids don't just learn driving from you. They learn how to read you while they drive. And my face was not a calm dashboard indicator back then. It was a flashing warning light.

Borderline Horrific Moment #1: "You Almost Killed Pops!"

There's an odd intersection as you wind through southwest Gaston County heading toward Crowders Mountain. It's a three-way intersection that must have been a paved-over horse path at some time because it makes no navigational sense. I've almost messed it up myself before.

That's important. Because on the way in, I started to get a little tense inside, but I didn't say anything. That's how 1.0 works. You don't say what you feel; you just tighten and hope the other person magically drives through your nervous system.

Here's the intersection in human words: As you approach

from the south, the west has a stop. The east has an option to veer left or south or just keep heading straight west. It's as confusing as it sounds.

He wanted to veer left. He could see a car yielding at that odd yield. We had a yield too. And then I saw it. A car flying from our right not doing the veer. Not slowing. Going straight, right where we wanted to go.

I could see Owen wasn't yielding. I could see he was committed. I could see the collision before it became a collision. Owen looked up and maybe sensed or hoped the guy to the right would too.

He didn't. He was going about forty and Owen about thirty, and at the absolute last moment, I don't think I screamed an instruction or anything, I just yelled "FUCK!"

Not elegant. Not instructional. Pure nervous system. Luckily, Owen knew what to do and smashed the brakes. The guy drove on. Stunned, I turned left and exclaimed:

"You almost killed Pops!"

Owen was equally stunned. He paused, looked me square in the eye, and said, deadpan:

"I know."

No defensiveness. No panic. Just truth. That sentence should have been a turning point. It wasn't. Because 1.0 doesn't learn from moments like that.

Borderline Horrific Moment #2: "We Almost Got Crushed!"

There's another odd intersection near the middle school, a busy one off New Hope Road. There's a bleed-in merge to turn left onto a wide four-lane road leading up to the school. A senior development and a church up the road only add to the hectic pace. Everyone is either late, distracted, or both.

As Owen decided it was his time to veer and merge left to head toward the middle school, a big silver Suburban was doing all it could to make the light before getting stuck again on New Hope.

Owen kind of hit the gas hard and braked at the same time. The big Suburban lurched to a stop right at my door and Connor's door behind me. We sat stunned. And Connor and I blurted out the same thing at the same time:

"We almost got crushed."

That line became ours for some time after that. Not just for driving. For grades, relationships, jobs, travel. When something came close to going bad but didn't get to define the whole story, we'd drop it. "We almost got crushed." Then we'd exhale and move forward. It's pure 2.0, actually. Name the fear. Don't let it eat the rest of the night. But in that season, I wasn't living there yet. In that season, I treated fear like a project.

How I Jammed His Radar

Here's the part that took me years to see clearly: I wasn't making Owen safer. I was making him anxious. Every correction landed as doubt. Every warning trained his nervous system to scan instead of drive. I flooded him with information and stripped him of intuition. I didn't trust the road. I didn't trust other drivers. And underneath it all I didn't trust him.

That's hard to admit because I love him. Of course I do. I would do anything for my kids without a second thought. So it's uncomfortable to realize that love doesn't automatically mean your frequency is clean.

Sometimes love comes out as control. Sometimes it comes out as commentary. Sometimes it comes out as a dad narrating everything because silence makes him feel irresponsible. Owen felt my frequency before he understood my words.

And because I was ahead of the moment—emotionally preloaded, tightened, scanning—he started driving that way too.

The Accidents and the Quiet Math

I wish these were just the chuckle-ha-ha driver's ed stories you tell later when the family gets together. They weren't. Luckily, Owen has always worn his seat belt and isn't a speeder. So it's "just car damage." But the numbers don't lie. He's had numerous accidents.

The first was a car he shared with his brother and sister. That was a poor deer on Ridgefall Road. You tell your kid they're okay, and you're relieved … and then the dad brain starts running the spreadsheet. Tow truck. Insurance claim. Deductible. Premiums. Points. The cost of freedom.

Then one afternoon at my old place on Pam Drive, I noticed my Maxima had mud all over the grill. *No biggie*, I thought. I grabbed the hose. But as I started spraying, I saw cracks. More damage. Misalignment. The kind of damage you don't notice until you stop pretending it's fine.

Owen had gotten ice cream the night before. He told me nonchalantly—and this is Owen, so the nonchalant tone was almost comical—that he thought he'd hit someone.

An insurance deductible later, the Maxima had an $8,000 facelift. New equipment. New parts. New reminder that teaching a kid to drive isn't just teaching. It's the slow handoff of cost, consequence, and responsibility. Then there was one more wreck. And then another—this one totaling the car—on his way to our summer retreat in Cheraw in 2025.

Each accident came with its own paperwork, its own awkward silence, its own "are you okay?" But what stuck with me wasn't the money. It was the pattern. And the uncomfortable question underneath it. How much of this is him … and how much is the frequency I put in the air.

FIELD NOTES
Fatherhood Physics

Your kids feel your emotional frequency before
they understand your words.
When you tune yourself, you tune the entire car.

The Apology That Rewired Everything

One afternoon, Owen and I were in the car together and the words finally showed up. It was the kind of drive I've come to love—ordinary, unhurried, the two of us moving through familiar roads with nothing to prove. Owen was driving the way I'd hoped he would: steady, smooth, present. And for once, the air in the car felt like it belonged to both of us.

That's when I felt it—the quiet space where truth can actually land. "Man … all that bad driving stuff? That was on me." No add-ons. No explanations. No "but." Just ownership. Owen didn't make a thing out of it. He didn't take a victory lap. He didn't pile on.

He just smiled—small, quiet, grateful. Like a kid who's been waiting for his dad to see the whole picture. And then he kept driving.

Here's how I knew the shift was real: For the first time in years, he didn't glance over to read my mood. He just drove—clean, relaxed, untightened. He trusted the air between us.

That's not a small thing. A father awakening isn't loud. It's a recalibration. A nervous system that doesn't make your kid flinch. That's the inheritance.

NOTES FROM A DIVORCED DAD
What to Carry Forward

- Overcorrection usually comes from fear, not incompetence
- The body teaches faster than the mouth
- Calm hands and a calm voice regulate more than instructions do

- When you tighten, the whole car feels it, especially the passenger
- The correction isn't "drive better," it's "be here"

STEADINESS IS CONTAGIOUS

How Calm Gets Taught

For a long time, I thought steadiness was just a personality trait—something some men had and others didn't. I didn't yet understand it as something transmissible, or costly in its absence. That took time. And it took watching a few men up close.

Before I get to them, I need to show you where I first learned to name what steadiness saved me from—not as a concept, but as a lived daily cost.

It didn't arrive as a lesson. It arrived as a moment in my own life when the lights dimmed, the crowd noise faded, and I was finally alone with the version of myself I'd been performing.

Some men turn back. Some men sprint ahead. I didn't do either. I stopped long enough to look in the mirror.

That amazing woman I met during Covid once told me:

Some people think because they don't support you, it'll hold you back… Let me tell you, God will put total strangers in your path to get you where you're supposed to be.

At the time, I thought she meant herself. Now I know she meant someone else entirely. She meant Stella.

It was one of those late trade-show nights where your jaw is still moving even though the floor's been closed for an hour. The carpet felt sticky and tired. The lights were half-dimmed. The last customers drifted off with tote bags and lanyards while every vendor fought the same internal monologue: "If one more guy asks about tow size, I'm going to walk into traffic."

Stella and I walked out of the hall like many shows before, bleary eyed and done. We had that dazed, post-conference shuffle—badge lanyards wound around fingers, rolling cases rattling behind us. "I swear my jaw is still bobbling like a dashboard bobblehead," I said. She laughed that signature Stella laugh. "Bless your heart, honey. That's sales."

We found the hotel bar, the standard-issue one. Weak downlighting. Worn leather stools. A bartender who looked like he'd invented disappointment.

Stella is Southern smart. Not resume smart—human smart. She sees people in one beat and acts on the second. She's warm and sharp and earthy. She's also seasoned, the kind of woman who can carry a room with a laugh, and carry her own life with a quiet spine you don't see unless you're paying attention.

Over years of travel, flights, booth setups, and factory floors, she became one of the very few people who got the real me. Not "how's travel?" honesty. Not "what's the forecast?" honesty. Actual honesty.

And that mattered because this was in the era where everything was piling up: kids, divorce fallout, exhaustion, money squeeze, corporate politics, and an ulcer—including a hotel bathroom telemedicine call where Dr. Geyer prescribed Prevacid and Phenergan just to get me home without ending up in the emergency room.

In those stretches, the question isn't "how do I get through this?" It's "who actually sees me in this?" For me, for a while, that person was Stella. Two drinks in, the Sunday-school filter dropped and real language took over—the salty, honest version of being alive.

We started joking about how fake we had to be all day. Not fraudulent fake. Not liar fake. Survival fake. The kind where your stomach is on fire and your kid's hurting and your bank account is a circus, but you're still smiling and asking some stranger if they've ever considered switching their composite supplier.

I quoted Tony Soprano: "Still I gotta be the sad clown."

Stella nodded with that look that says "Yeah, I've been there."

We sat in it for a moment, letting the truth of it breathe. And then the line finally arrived—simple, accurate, impossible to take back.

"You know what's more sinister than the Twilight Zone?" I said. She raised an eyebrow.

"Its twisted cousin—the Fakery Zone!"

She laughed out loud. And then we kept going—back and forth, naming it from every angle, circling it for nearly an hour. We named it, and the naming felt like oxygen.

What is the Fakery Zone? It's not lying. It's not deception. It's the zone where you perform being okay, where you edit yourself just enough to keep the day moving. Your smile shows up two beats ahead of your soul. It's professionalism. It's courtesy. It's coping.

FIELD NOTES

How Honest Are You Really?

Honesty has settings.

- Some people get the full sentence
- Some people get the shortened version
- Some people get the weather report

Becoming steady isn't telling everybody everything.

It's knowing who has earned the real you—and giving that version where it heals instead of where it gets used.

So take a quick inventory:

- Your spouse or partner—do they get all of you, or the version that keeps the peace?
- Your boss—do they get the confident performer or the exhausted human wondering "How long can I keep doing this"?
- Your kids—do they get your heart or your highlight reel?
- Your friends—who knows the real battle you're fighting?

- Yourself—can you look in the mirror and tell yourself the unedited truth?

Reduce fakery by five percent this week. Just five.
One sentence. One honest response. One—
"Actually? It's been a rough week."

Here's the part about the Fakery Zone that mattered to Stella, and ended up mattering to me. That performance costs something. She called it the editing tax. And once you name the mask, you can choose when to wear it—instead of waking up one day realizing it has fused to your face.

Stella didn't fix me. She did something better. She made truth feel normal, and that sense of oxygen lingered long after we left the room. Once you feel that difference, you start noticing the men who don't live in the Fakery Zone at all. Men like Grant.

Grant S.–The Strong Spine OG

Grant is a self-made millionaire. You would never know it if you met him. Worn-out Chevy Tahoe filled with boxes of old proposals, drawings, back-of-the-napkin sketches. Maybe one of the most driven, hardworking men you will ever meet. Bar none. Hard stop.

He owned a composite company with his partner, Jeff, and the company was headed toward the kind of payday most people coast into. If there's ever a time to let your foot off the gas, it's when the finish line is in sight and you've already won. Not Grant.

I'd leave the office around 8:30 on a Wednesday night, feeling guilty, heading home to my wife and three young ones. Three kids in diapers in those days. Grant never once said, "Stay, we need to do more." He didn't have to. The way he carried himself made you want to stay. Made you want to outlast him. That was impossible.

Jeff (The Other Half of the Machine)

Grant had the spine and the ability to sell, and people trusted him quickly. Jeff had this one-of-a-kind blend of deep technical knowledge and strong business acumen. Together they were a formidable pair, the kind you only see a few times in a career. Not because they were flashy, but because they were integrated. No gaps between what they knew and what they produced.

When I left the company, I wrote Jeff a note about that. He was a little annoyed at me leaving for my new job, so I don't know if he ever read it. But I meant it. And the thing I learned from watching them wasn't just "how to negotiate" or "how to build a company."

It was that you can be firm and still be compassionate. You can push and still be human. You can demand excellence without humiliating people to get it. That's a rare mix. That's a new form of masculinity before I could name it.

The Program That Put Them on the Map

The program that really put the company on the map—and led to them selling it—was producing composite components for a next-generation platform. It was a massive program that ran for many years. The major prime that won the contract designed the system from the ground up, integrated all the components, and awarded subcontracts to companies like Grant's.

Here's the part that people outside aerospace don't always understand. Programs like this are long games. It can take ten-plus years just to reach full rate production.

And even if you're "in," nothing is guaranteed. Any disruption in performance can influence your role in the supply chain when it gets to production, and that is when the real profit is made.

So yes, the company was in an enviable position. But it was still nerve-wracking. This wasn't like signing a big software deal where the contract hits, the money is paid, and everyone pops champagne. This was a slow build with real consequences, real scrutiny, real pressure.

"Jeff … Maybe We Better Get an Early Flight"

It was a long day. Negotiations for the major program had turned serious, and the prime finally put a number on the table for the composite components Grant and Jeff's firm would produce.

They likely had that number at the start of the day. But this is aerospace. Which means it takes hours of micro-details and squabbles to get to the part everyone came for. Songs and dances. Posturing. The little theater people do when the room feels too high-stakes to just tell the truth. You know, the Fakery Zone.

Grant looked at the number. You would think he'd be worn down by now. There had been a parade of people in and out all day. The kind of day where you feel your brain start to soften around the edges.

Grant just stared at it. Then he looked at Jeff, deadpan, and said the words that made them both millions. "Jeff … maybe we better get an early flight." Nothing else.

Here's what I remember that I didn't have language for back then: My body copied him.

My breathing had been shallow all day—conference breathing, negotiation breathing—chest doing the work while my stomach stayed locked like a fist.

When Grant said it calmly, almost kindly, something in my nervous system unclenched without permission. My shoulders dropped half an inch. My jaw stopped grinding. And I watched the guys across the table do it too. A room full of grown men, supposedly in control, recalibrating to one steady man like iron filings to a magnet.

That's what I mean when I say steadiness is contagious. It doesn't convince you. It infects you. And there was a look Grant gave Jeff right after he said it—Soft Eyes, no ego, no performance. Just two men who trusted each other enough to let silence do some of the work.

No overcorrecting. No smoothing. No trying to read the room and adjust his tone to keep everyone comfortable. Just silence, the words hanging in the air like a fart in an elevator. That's Strong Spine in action.

When someone pushed back, Grant didn't counterpunch. He simply repeated himself calmly, almost kindly, like he was stating the weather. There was no edge. No tension. Nothing to push against. And the room would adjust. At the time, I didn't analyze it. I just clocked it.

Not aggression. Not bluffing. Presence. The room tightened and then adjusted. One of the senior guys finally said something like, "Okay … how can we make it work?" Typical. Middle number. Split the difference. Call it a day.

Grant didn't overreach. He didn't grandstand. He didn't explain the deal into the ground. He just rolled up his sleeves and said, essentially, "What if we made more parts?" Light bulb.

The next two days were spent with engineers and designers expanding the scope from a couple components to eleven highly engineered, high-value, system-ready assemblies. That one sentence changed the deal. It also gave me a blueprint I wouldn't understand until years later.

The real lesson wasn't negotiation tactics. It was a nervous system lesson. Grant wasn't performing competence. He was inhabiting it. Back then, I didn't see him as a model. I saw him as an outlier. Someone who had earned the right to be calm. Someone who could afford to be unbothered. Someone operating under different rules. I assumed I'd get there eventually. In the meantime, I stayed busy in the places I felt fluent.

FIELD NOTES
Strong Spine in Practice

Strong Spine looks like:

- Saying less, not more
- Letting silence do some of the work
- Holding the line without clenching your jaw
- Repeating yourself calmly instead of escalating
- Being firm without humiliating people to prove it

- If you feel the urge to over-explain, check your spine

The Sticky One

Ben is one of those guys you meet in your career who is just … sticky. You always stay in touch somehow. Not super close. We know just enough about each other to be dangerous. It helps that we're about the same age—he's a little younger, with a kind of easy, ageless energy—and we grew up in the same southeastern Massachusetts area. We share a language without needing to explain it.

But the main bond is simple. We both worked for Grant. We survived him. And when I say "survived Grant," I mean it in the affectionate, respectful way you talk about a coach who was demanding as hell but made you better.

Ben was a plant manager in those days. Capable in office roles, sales roles, whatever you needed, but he was a shop guy at heart. Comfortable with his people. Comfortable with the floor. Comfortable with the reality of work instead of the performance of it.

Eventually Ben took a huge step out of his comfort zone and started his own composites parts company with his partners Brian and Jim. Fifteen years in, they're still standing. That alone deserves respect.

I don't think they're "killing it" yet, not in the fantasy "sold it, bought a boat, moved to the Cape" way, but they're doing damn good. They've got big programs that they work, and I'm genuinely rooting for them. Because building something real is always worth rooting for.

The Pocket Outside the Zone

CAMX is the annual big composites show in North America. This year it was in Orlando. I was there with my current team. We did the usual big show thing—a full week of meetings, trade-show floor, and dinners. Someday someone will tell me if it was ever worth all the time I spent at trade shows. But this one matters. It is the largest my company does.

By the end days at CAMX, your head is full and your guard is up. Every conversation feels slightly performative, even the honest ones. But sometimes, even at CAMX, the fakery drops for a moment.

On this trip, like some others, Ben and some of the old guys who used to work for Grant were in Orlando. We met up at a bar not too far from the convention center. My buddy Matt was already there, along with one of Ben's partners, Brian. And for an hour or so, we were back at that old plant in Massachusetts.

It sounds ridiculous, but it was like wrapping yourself in a cozy blanket for a moment. No sad-clown time. Just men who didn't need to explain themselves before speaking. Voices drop back into their natural register. Shoulders loosen. Stories wander without needing a point. And I was comfortable there. Which is why what happened next mattered.

The Question (And the Third-Person Slip)

At some point, Ben, beer in hand, finishing a big laugh, turned to me and got serious. He started asking me work questions. Real ones. He was nervous about a big proposal they were working on and needed a soft sounding board. One without an agenda. One that wouldn't be unnecessarily critical. One that would just be present.

And here's where my sales training finally did something useful beyond making money. I listened. A good sales guy always listens first. Selling can wait. Listen and really hear what the person is saying, in life and in work. You'd be surprised what you can learn when you shut your mouth.

When he finished, I had the entire answer mapped out in my mind. Notice I didn't say the right answer. Just my answer. But in sales, confidence is king. And maybe in life too. Calm confidence. So I started explaining and then this sentence slipped out:

"This is what Eric would do."

Ben didn't react. Ben nodded. Then he suddenly started laughing and asked:

"Did you just refer to yourself in the third person?"

He wasn't going to miss the chance to bust my balls and ask if I'd just had a George-likes-his-chicken-spicy moment. But we just laughed, and I kept on with my opinion. Whether he really wanted it is a different story. I think he just wanted a safe place to vent.

The conversation kept moving. Nothing broke. But something inside me paused. It wasn't shame. It wasn't panic. It wasn't embarrassment. It was curiosity. I remember thinking: *Huh, that's interesting.*

Why didn't I just say what I would do?

I'd spoken about myself in the third person, as if I were slightly removed from my own experience—standing just off to the side of it. It was subtle. It worked. It kept things smooth. And it was familiar.

That night in Orlando, the realization didn't land like a verdict. It landed like a note to myself. Pay attention to this. Not to fix it. Not to eradicate it. Just to notice when I stepped outside myself instead of standing where I was.

That's how awakening actually starts. Not with revelation. With recognition.

The Bro Code Benediction

We wrapped up our brief visit before the last stretch of work and dinners with customers and suppliers—a quick "good seeing you, brother. Don't be a stranger."

We all laughed. We all knew what it meant. Connection without performance. Affection without explanation.

But we still had real work to do. Customers waiting. Late Teams calls. The grind resumes. I hopped in my rental car and headed down Independence Drive, thinking about that spicy-chicken moment.

Up ahead at a stoplight, Ben, Matt, and Brian were waiting for the light to change. I was going to drive right past them. So I did what emotionally healthy men do when they don't know how to be emotionally healthy in public. I rolled down the window, made eye contact, and shouted "Fuck you!" Big grin. Middle finger. Pure bro code.

Driving away, I could see them realize *oh shit, that was Brockman* with huge smiles on their faces. In 2.0, you can say "I love you." You still wrap it in humor.

The Real Lesson

Strong Spine isn't domination. It isn't winning arguments. It isn't controlling outcomes. It's being so steady you don't need to rush, perform, or explain yourself into relevance.

Grant had it long before I knew what to call it. Jeff had it in a different form—a quiet competence that didn't need applause. Ben is learning it in real time, building something, quoting big programs, staying in the arena long enough to earn his own win.

And me? I was beginning to realize masculinity isn't about choosing between hard and soft. It's about integration. Like an engineered composite. Not a monolithic hunk of metal, but strength in some places, stiffness in others, flexibility where the load demands it. A tuned system. Not a performance. A build.

And then there's Stella. Steadiness shows up in more ways than we expect. Sometimes a total stranger enters your life not to teach you anything, but to give you a place where the mask can come off.

That kind of steadiness counts. It doesn't instruct. It doesn't correct. It just gives you room to breathe—and reminds you what honesty feels like when it's finally safe.

NOTES FROM A DIVORCED DAD
What to Carry Forward

- Masculinity is caught more than it's taught
- The best men transmit steadiness without speeches
- Real strength often looks quieter than you expect
- You become what you spend time around
- Borrow what's clean. Leave what's tightened.

LAND CLEARING AND THE REBUILDING OF A MAN

Working Without an Audience

Land doesn't lie. Neither does your nervous system. Some awakenings are loud. A blow-up. A blowout. A bottom. A headline. A door that closes hard enough to rattle the whole house. Mine wasn't like that. Mine was a slow, unglamorous regrading. A season where the loudest thing in my life was not a conversation but a line of heavy machines chewing through a stretch of woods on New Hope Road while I sat in my car like I was in a confessional.

No one knew I was doing it. No one would have cared. That's not self-pity. That's just the truth of how men change. Most of it happens out of frame. And the parts that happen out of frame are usually the parts that last. I can still see the morning light in my driveway. That blue-grey Carolina pre-sunrise that makes everything look honest because it hasn't been warmed up yet. Connor was asleep inside.

The house was quiet in that way that feels like permission. Gym towel in hand. And the familiar old voice in my head already starting up: Don't screw today up. Don't miss anything. Don't forget anyone. Don't fall behind. Don't let anybody down.

Eric 1.0 didn't wake up "sad." He woke up at times locked up. He woke up like he was late to a fire. Even when nothing was burning. And the weird thing about bracing is you stop noticing it. You think it's just how you are. You think it's your personality. You think it's strength. Until you sit on the side of a road at 6:45 a.m. and watch a forest come down with more calm than you've had in ten years. Then you realize: *Oh. I'm the one who's loud.*

The Road That Started Talking

I started noticing New Hope Road the way you notice a bruise you forgot you had. You don't remember the impact. But there it is, tender, purple, undeniable. At first it was small. Orange fencing. Long, bright, almost comical. Like somebody took a highlighter to the side of the world. It didn't ask permission. It didn't explain itself. It didn't apologize. It just showed up and said: "This is the line now." I remember liking how clean that was. A boundary with no emotion attached to it. Pure function.

A few days later I found the map online of what the land was about to become: improvements from Union New Hope Road down to Titman Road. The same stretch I'd been driving on for years. What was nothing but stretches of pine tree forest suddenly looked like a plan. Lane lines, turn pockets, right-of-way edges, little legends and symbols that mean something to engineers and almost nothing to the rest of us.

But even if you don't speak "DOT," you can read intent. The colors were the message: This is where it widens, this is where it shifts, this is where it gets serious. That's what hit me. Real rebuilding happens on paper first. Somebody has to decide what's coming down, where the new line goes, and how much mess they're willing to tolerate to get there.

I'd been telling myself I wanted a new life, a calmer life, a stronger-spine life. But I was still secretly hoping it could happen without demolition. Without inconvenience. Without the "between" season where everything looks worse.

The map didn't offer that fantasy. It just offered the truth: You want a new road, you're going to live through torn-up shoulder, orange fencing, mud days, detours, and red clay season.

Meanwhile my whole adult life had been the opposite. Emotion attached to everything. Even boundaries. Especially boundaries. I was the guy who could turn "no" into a paragraph. The guy who could turn "I can't" into a trial brief. The guy who could make a boundary sound like an apology for existing. A man trying to hold his spine while simultaneously taking responsibility for everybody else's feelings about his spine.

Then the piles showed up. Red clay stacked like somebody had emptied the earth's pockets onto the shoulder. Dirt, broken roots, crushed leaves, a few stunned pine limbs still green at the ends like they didn't get the memo. It looked like damage. It looked like somebody lost. It looked like the kind of place people went when they didn't want to feel anything.

And that's the part people forget about rebuilding: It looks like destruction while it's happening. You'll want to rush past it.

You'll want to rename it. "Progress." "Development." "New construction." Something that sounds clean. But you can't rename it. Red clay doesn't care what you call it.

The First Morning I Pulled Over

At first I would drive past. The first morning I pulled over, I didn't do it because I had a plan. I did it because my body told me to. I was headed to the gym like I had been doing recently—early, quiet, no one around to witness me trying to become a steadier man.

Same route. Same half-awake stare men get when they're moving through their day by habit. Same playlist designed to drown out thinking. Then I came around that bend and saw the first real machines. Not a pickup truck. Not a backyard tractor. The big stuff. Tree-clearing machines that look like they were out of a *Mad Max* movie.

The kind of equipment that doesn't look like it moves. It looks like it arrives. And something in my chest did that small, familiar drop. Not panic. Not grief. That little internal fall like a step you didn't see. The one I used to ignore. The one I used to call "nothing." I pulled onto the shoulder like I'd been summoned. Blinker. Ease off the road. Gravel under tires. Put the car in park. Hands resting on the wheel. Engine still running. I remember how quiet it was inside the car. Like the car itself was holding its breath. Outside, the machines were not holding their breath. Outside was diesel rumble and steel clank and that backup alarm that sounds like every construction site in America.

Beep. Beep. Beep. A dozer blade leaned forward, slow, patient, inevitable. It met the edge of the woods and the woods didn't argue. Trees didn't negotiate. They didn't offer a compromise. They didn't tell the dozer about their childhood. They didn't say, "Hey, can we circle back on this later?"

The machine just pressed in. And the forest gave way. One tree went. Then another. Then a cluster. Not in a dramatic crash like in movies. More like a surrender. A heavy bend. A final crack. Then the sound of needles and limbs folding into each other like wet paper. I sat there with my water in hand and felt something I hadn't felt in a long time. Not sadness. Not rage. Not even hope. Recognition. This is what it looks like when something bigger than your story moves through what you've been protecting. This is what it looks like when the old version comes down.

What Most People See vs. What a Man in Transition Sees

Most people driving by saw a development project. Some complained about traffic. Some made a joke about "more houses." Some didn't notice at all. But a man in transition sees different things.

A man in transition starts to think back at things in his life that were signs of change. Signs that a new lens was available if he had the awareness to understand. The house on Pam Drive was my original land clearing. This was the early days of Covid, and the Pam Drive house was out in the beautiful part of Gaston County not many people get out to. The old-school southwest portion with horse farms and rolling hills. Nestled in between are many single-level homes built before the Charlotte area boom times.

My rental house was one of these. It was pretty and quiet,

but the trees and brush on the property were wildly overgrown. I didn't realize it then, but this was my original land clearing. It was mild compared to what I would later see on New Hope Road—a land clearing beyond description. Machines I didn't even know existed.

A man in transition really watches the machines. He sees how the machines operate with full power and don't need to perform. They don't pose. They don't announce. You notice the people who operate those machines. They don't care if anyone understands the plan. They show up. They do the work. They go home. No emotional speeches. No grand narrative. No identity crisis. Just force applied in the right direction, at the right time, for long enough.

I watched those machines and felt my own recent life start to make sense. Because that season wasn't a cinematic "before and after." It was a lot of mornings. A lot of small decisions. A lot of rewiring that no one could see. The kind of change that doesn't feel heroic while you're in it. It feels private. It feels ordinary. It feels like you're failing at being the old you … because the old you was built on drawing tight. And you're trying to stop pulling tight.

That's not a glamorous skill. It's a quiet one. It's you in your kitchen at 10:30 p.m. choosing not to send the extra text. It's you in a conversation, feeling your old reflex to explain and choosing not to. It's you letting someone be disappointed without sprinting to fix it. It's you sitting with silence without stuffing it full of activity.

On the outside, it looks like nothing. On the inside, it's a demolition.

The G70 as a Confession Booth

I didn't plan on the Genesis being part of the story. It's just a car. But you know how certain objects become accidental confession booths? A shower. A front porch step. A particular chair. The driver's seat. The place where you finally stop talking and let your body say what it's been holding.

That G70 was mine. Leather seats, clean lines, all the premium stuff that's supposed to make a man feel like he's doing fine. And there I was, sitting in it. Not broken. Not falling apart. Just awake. That's the word. Awake. Awake to how much of my life had been performance management.

Me trying to drive the room like it was a car. Me trying to anticipate every turn so nobody would feel a bump. Me trying to be such a "good man" that no one would ever have to say I wasn't. That's a version of good that will slowly kill you. It doesn't kill you with drama. It kills you with exhaustion.

And the scary part is you won't even call it exhaustion. You'll call it responsibility. You'll call it leadership. You'll call it "doing what needs to be done." Until one morning you're on the side of New Hope Road watching a dozer push a forest over and you realize: *I've been bracing my whole life.*

The Men Who Run the Machines

Every now and then I'd catch a glimpse of the operators, hands on controls, doing something violent with astonishing calm. No speeches. No grand narrative. Just work. I'd think about how little of their emotion entered the machine. They weren't mad.

They weren't hyped. They weren't performing masculinity. They were executing. Competence. Presence. Regulation.

It reminded me of a kind of masculinity I'd always respected but didn't know how to inhabit. The quiet kind. The kind my father had in flashes when he wasn't being a salesman, when he was just being a man doing a job. I can still picture my dad's hands on a steering wheel. Not white-knuckled. Not theatrical.

Just hands. Just control. Just "we're going to get there." That's the kind of steadiness I wanted. Not the kind that comes from suppressing emotion. The kind that comes from not dumping your emotion onto other people. I didn't want to become a tougher man. I wanted to become a truer one.

The Emotional Frequency of Heavy Machines

Here's the strange truth. Those machines felt calming. Not because destruction is calming. Because the machines were regulated. They weren't frantic. They weren't reactive. They didn't overcorrect. They didn't flinch. They didn't need to be admired. They did what they were built to do with a kind of slow certainty my body recognized as safety.

I didn't have language for this then. I hadn't turned it into a framework yet. But I can say it now: My body was responding to steadiness. To weight. To sequence. To the simple idea that you can move heavy things without losing your mind. That's what I was trying to become. A man who could move heavy things without losing his mind.

Not a man who never feels. Not a man who never shakes. A man who doesn't hand his shaking to his kids. A man who holds his own wheel. A man who can walk through the day with Soft

Eyes and a Strong Spine. And when I watched those machines—steady, loud, indifferent to opinions—I felt a clean conviction rise in me: This is how it's supposed to be. Not the destruction part. The steadiness part. The "show up and do the work" part. The "no performance" part.

The Boy Watching the Man's Work

There's always a boy inside a man like me. A Boston kid who learned early that staying sharp was the same thing as staying safe. A kid who thought tension meant readiness. A kid who got really good at overcorrecting.

That boy watched the land clearing and felt the same thing he felt watching strong men when he was young. A pull. But this time it wasn't the pull toward armor. It was the pull toward competence. Toward calm capability. Toward masculinity that isn't loud. Masculinity that doesn't need to win. Masculinity that can handle weight.

I didn't want to be the guy who talks about manhood. I wanted to be the guy who lives it. Quietly. Daily. In small ways that compound. So I kept pulling over. And more importantly, I started to look at my own life the way I was looking at the land—what was overgrown, what needed clearing, and what was already solid.

Not every day. But enough. Enough that the road became a ritual. New Hope Road wasn't just a place. It was a checkpoint. A weekly scan of the outer world that kept telling me the truth about the inner one.

When the Land Started Speaking Back

The next phase wasn't the machines. It was what the machines revealed. Roots. That's the part that got me. Because you don't really understand a forest until you see the underground system. Up top it looks like trunks and branches. Below it's a whole other story. Thick veins wrapped around other thick veins. A net of survival. A map of old storms.

Watching them yank roots up felt … personal. Because that's what rebuilding does. It exposes the stuff you were standing on. It drags up the patterns you inherited: The reflexes you called personality. The survival mechanisms you called leadership. The habits you called love.

This is where a lot of men quit. They'll do surface change. They'll clean up a behavior. They'll fix the schedule. They'll buy the book. They'll say the right words. But when the root system comes up? When they have to admit, "Oh … this isn't just a habit. This is how I learned to survive?" That's when men get embarrassed. That's when they want to rename it. That's when they want to rush. But the land doesn't rush. And healing that lasts doesn't rush either.

Red Clay Season

One morning, the sky was rinsed clear, the kind you only get when the air is cold and honest. No haze. No softness. Just a crisp line between heaven and earth. And down below it was all red. Raw clay. The stuff you track into your car if you step wrong. The stuff that stains your shoes like a reminder. The stuff you can't pretend isn't there. If you live in this part of the

Southeast, this is what you think dirt is, but to the rest of the country its unique.

A grader pushed that clay forward, blade low, consistent, smoothing a future I couldn't see yet. And I remember thinking, without trying to make it a metaphor: *This is what it feels like inside me right now.* Because I wasn't having a grand transformation. I was having a slow one.

The kind where you don't even know you've changed until you hear your own voice in a moment that used to set you off. The kind where you don't realize you've been regraded until you stop reacting like you used to. The kind where your kids walk in and the air in the room feels different.

Not because you said anything new. Because you are something new. And the land kept showing me the same truth on repeat: Before you can build anything, you have to disturb what's been sitting there. Before you can pour a foundation, you have to admit what the ground is.

Before you can make a clean line, you have to cut through the messy part. That's not inspirational. That's just reality.

The Day I Didn't Send the Text

Here's a tiny scene that would never make a movie. But it's the kind of scene a man is made of. I had one of those exchanges— nothing explosive, nothing dramatic—just a moment where my old reflex lit up. Explain. Correct. Clarify. Make sure they understand you're not the bad guy. Make sure the story doesn't tilt against you.

I had the phone in my hand. I had the words half-typed. My thumbs were already moving like they were on rails. And then, for whatever reason, my mind flashed to New Hope Road. Not the road itself. The orange fencing. The piles. The blade. The steadiness. And I felt the question land clean: Do you want to clear … or do you want to keep planting trees?

Over-texting is a form of planting. You plant words, hoping they grow into control. You plant explanations, hoping they grow into safety. You plant emotional labor, hoping it grows into someone else's comfort. And sometimes the strongest thing you can do is not plant another tree.

So I deleted the text. Put the phone down. Let the discomfort exist. And that day, quietly, I moved a root. Nobody clapped. Nobody knew. But something in me shifted. That's how this new man was being built. One un-sent text at a time.

The Burn Piles

Then came the burn piles. If you've never seen them up close, you won't understand why they matter. They aren't pretty. They're not a "fresh start." They're the ugly inventory of what had to come down. Broken branches. Old logs. Twisted roots. Half-green pine tops that still smell like Christmas but look like they got dragged out by their hair.

Stacks and stacks of a former life. And the burn piles just sat there. Waiting. Like the land was saying, "We're not done with this yet. We're going to deal with all of it. Not just the parts you want to talk about." This was the moment I stopped trying to keep my past tidy.

I stopped being the guy who says, "It wasn't that bad." I stopped being the guy who forgives too fast so no one thinks he's bitter. I stopped being the guy who can explain every conflict so smoothly that people forget it hurt. Because the burn piles don't explain. They just exist. And eventually they burn.

Not with drama. With heat. With finality. With smoke you can see from miles away. That's the part men don't talk about. The part where you let something die. Not because you hate it. Because you're done living inside it.

Mud Days

Not every day was blue sky and clean symbolism. Some mornings it rained. Heavy rain that turns red clay into a slick, stubborn paste. The whole site would look like a wound. Truck tracks filled with water. Boot prints everywhere. A kind of messy, half-finished ugliness that made it hard to imagine "nice neighborhood" or "new homes" or anything polished.

And that's the other part of rebuilding nobody posts. The mud days. The days when you're doing the work and it doesn't look like progress. The days when everything is slippery. The days when you feel like you're going backwards. Those were the days I related to the project most.

Because my own rebuild didn't feel like a steady climb. It felt like two steps forward, one step back. Sometimes two. A good week of calm. Then one bad morning when my old anxiety tried to take the wheel. A clean boundary held … then a moment of over-explaining because I got tired. A day when I did great, then a night when I stared at my phone like it was a live wire.

That's the mud. That's not failure. That's the middle. And the men who make it through the middle are the men who stop calling the mud a verdict. They call it weather. They keep moving.

The Steady Work Nobody Cheers For

There's a kind of masculinity that's built in private. No audience. No "look at me." No motivational quotes. Just repetition. Just showing up. Just doing the thing that makes you better, even when nobody sees it. That's what those mornings became for me. Gym. Work. Kids. Bills. Life. And tucked inside all that, a few minutes on the shoulder of New Hope Road, watching progress happen the slow way.

I'd sit there and let my breathing match the machines. Slow inhale. Slow exhale. Beep-beep of a truck backing up. Diesel rumble. Blade scrape. The soft collapse of brush. And I'd feel my own internal noise, usually loud, start to quiet. Not because my problems disappeared. Because I stopped fighting reality for a minute. I stopped narrating. I stopped pleading with the past. I just watched the truth unfold: A new thing takes time. A new man takes time.

The House as a Build Site

While all of that was happening out there, there was construction happening in my house, too. Not literal construction. The kind nobody gets permits for. The kind where you're rebuilding the atmosphere. I started paying attention to small things the way you pay attention when you've finally decided the details matter. The tone of my voice when the kids walked in. The speed of my answers. Whether I was listening to understand or listening to respond. Whether the house felt like a landing pad ... or a courtroom. I'd catch myself about to do the old move: ask three questions in a row, fill the silence, perform fatherhood like it was a job interview.

And then I'd slow down. Let the space breathe. Let the kids talk on their own schedule. Let the room be ordinary. It sounds small. It is small. And it's everything. Because kids don't remember the speech you gave. They remember what it felt like to be near you. They remember if your energy made them tense. They remember if they could exhale. So I started building a home that felt like an exhale. Not perfect. Not always. But more often. That's the kind of construction that matters. That's the kind of construction that lasts.

The Day Owen Came Home

Owen came home with his girlfriend for their first real visit. I can recall the excitement and the feeling in the air. I'd cleaned the house like I always do when my kids come over. Not in a desperate way. In a "let's make this place feel like a landing pad" way. Little details that say: "I thought of you."

They pulled up, and Owen stepped out with that familiar posture. Older now, but still my kid. There's always that first minute where you're trying not to overdo it. Trying not to make it a thing. Trying to be a steady man with a steady welcome.

We came inside. We talked. We laughed. We did the normal dance. And then, like a reflex, I blurted out: "Did you see what they're doing on New Hope Road?"

It came out fast and eager. I heard it as soon as it left my mouth. And I knew what I was really asking. I wasn't talking about bulldozers. I was asking: "Do you see me? Do you see that I'm changing? Do you see that I'm doing the work? Do you see that the man in front of you isn't the storm-dad you grew up with? Do you see the clearing?"

Owen looked at me with that half-smile he's had since he was little, the one that says he's clocking more than he's saying. "Yeah, Pops," he said. "It's wild."

Just that. No big speech. No emotional verdict. But I felt something in it. A small acknowledgment. A nod. A confirmation that I wasn't doing this in a vacuum.

That my sons could feel the difference, even if they didn't have the words for it. And I realized something right then: Your kids don't need you to explain your growth. They need to experience it. They don't need your manifesto. They need your tone. They need your steadiness. They need you to be the kind of man they can relax around.

The kind of man whose presence doesn't demand anything from them. The kind of man who doesn't make them carry his emotions. That's the clearing. Not the dirt on the roadside. The air inside the house.

The String Line

One morning I saw something that made me laugh, because it was so simple. A string line. Bright string pulled tight between stakes. A laser level tripod sitting there like a tiny robot priest.

Guys walking slow, checking measurements, calling out numbers like the future was a math problem. And I remember thinking, *This is what I've been missing.* Not more emotion. Not more analysis. A line. A measurement. A standard.

Because a man in transition can get addicted to feeling. He can become a professional "processor." He can confuse intensity with growth. But growth, real growth, often looks like a line pulled tight. A decision held. A boundary kept. A tone chosen.

A standard returned to on the days you don't feel like it. The string line made me want to stop making everything a referendum on my worth. It made me want to become the kind of man who can say: "This is the line." And then live like it's true.

Survey Stakes

Later, after months of disruption, the survey stakes started showing up. Little neon flags in the ground. Thin wooden posts with numbers. Tiny signals that said: "A plan exists. A future is being measured here. Not on your timeline. On reality's." And that's when the chapter turned for me.

Because it's one thing to be willing to demolish. A lot of men can do demolition. We can blow things up. We can burn bridges. We can make big changes out of pain.

But survey stakes are different. Survey stakes are patience. Survey stakes are intention. Survey stakes are quiet confidence that you're building toward something, not just running from something. That's what Part II of the book has been about for me.

Not "getting over" my life. Building a new one. Regrading my inner ground so the foundation holds. So the next chapter isn't just a repeat with different characters. So my kids don't have to inherit my tightening. So my masculinity stops being a costume and becomes a home.

FIELD NOTE
What the Machines Taught Me

Show up. Even when you don't feel ready.

Go slow. Slow is not weak.

Hold your line. A boundary doesn't need a sermon.

Move one thing at a time. Don't try to clear the whole forest in one day.

Respect sequence. First disruption. Then removal. Then grading. Then stakes. Then foundation.

Let the ugly middle be ugly. Don't rename it. Don't romanticize it. Just keep working.

Stop performing. Stop auditioning. Stop asking the world to clap.

Do the work. Go home. Sleep. Come back. That's how a man gets made.

The Last Morning

The last morning I pulled over the machines were still there, but the chaos wasn't. The line was straighter. The ground looked calmer. The piles were smaller. The work had moved from demolition to preparation.

And that's when it hit me: There's a moment in a man's transformation when the loud part ends. The crisis. The scramble. The "what happened to my life" phase. And something quieter begins.

A man starts living from the new grade. Not because he's done. Because he's ready.

I sat there for a few minutes and felt a different kind of stillness. Not numbness. Not resignation. Peace. The kind that comes from alignment. The kind that comes from finally being on your own side.

I put the car back in drive. Turned the wheel. And rejoined the road. And I drove into the next part of the book with a new truth humming under everything: Strength doesn't have to be armor. It can be softness with a spine. That's what I was finally learning.

The Quiet After the Machines

Toward the end, when most of the clearing was done, the site got quieter. Not silent. But quieter in a way you notice. More space. More sky. Less chaos. The birds started showing up again. Not as a symbol. As a fact.

And I realized something I didn't expect: I missed the noise. Not because I love noise. Because noise had become familiar. Noise had been my whole emotional life.

Chaos, urgency, reaction—those were my home languages.

So when the land got quiet, part of me didn't know what to do with it. That's a real thing in men. We say we want peace, but peace can feel like a foreign country at first.

Peace can feel like boredom. Peace can feel like vulnerability. Peace can feel like you're missing something until you realize what you're missing is the old addiction to tightening.

So I practiced letting the quiet be quiet. I practiced not filling it. I practiced letting my shoulders drop without waiting for the next shoe to fall. And that practice, more than any speech, more than any insight, was the making of a man.

Because the new masculinity I was heading into isn't about being tougher. It's about being real. Strong enough to stay soft. Steady enough to stay open. Present enough to let my kids breathe around me. That's where this road was taking me. Not to a new subdivision. To a new way of living.

NOTES FROM A DIVORCED DAD
What to Carry Forward

- Real rebuilding happens on paper first: a line, a measurement, a standard
- Don't confuse intensity with growth; growth often looks quiet
- A boundary doesn't need a sermon; it needs repetition
- Respect sequence: disruption—removal—grading—stakes—foundation
- Let the ugly middle be ugly—don't rename it, just keep working
- Your kids don't need your manifesto, they need your tone

PART III

STRENGTH WITHOUT ARMOR

Calm That Holds

This is the part where strength becomes something you live. It shows up as steadiness—quiet, grounded, and unconcerned with being seen or validated.

A lot of men were taught that softness is dangerous. That if you open your heart, you'll get punished for it. So they learn armor. Sarcasm. Withdrawal. Dominance. The cold stare. The raised voice that says "I'm not the one you get to question." It works in the short term. It makes people back up. But it doesn't make them feel safe. And it doesn't make you feel proud.

Soft Eyes isn't weakness. It's presence that makes people feel safe. Strong Spine isn't aggression. It's steadiness that keeps you from folding. When those two work together, you become a man who can lead without threat. You can listen without collapsing. You can set a boundary and still keep your dignity—and theirs.

This part is recalibration. The same man, less reactive. The same love, less desperate. The same authority, less heat. You'll learn how to stay in the room without taking over the room. You'll start building a calm that isn't passive—calm that holds.

If you've been living like you need armor to survive, this part will feel like taking a deep breath you didn't know you were allowed to take.

HOLDING THE LINE WITHOUT FIRE

Strength Without Armor

Is it possible to be soft and strong? For a long time, I thought softness meant collapse. I didn't have a word for it back then, but I could feel the fear underneath the idea. If I relaxed, something would fall. If I let go, I'd lose ground. If I softened, I'd stop being taken seriously as a man, as a father, as someone who could be counted on.

So I stayed firm. Alert. Ready. I mistook tension for strength and vigilance for leadership. It looked right from the outside. It even felt responsible. But it came with a cost I didn't know how to name at the time.

The cost was that everything had to move through me. Every emotion. Every decision. Every problem. Every silence. Healthy masculine softness didn't arrive as a revelation. It didn't show up in a conversation or a book or a sudden insight. It crept in slowly through posture more than thought. Through what I stopped doing before I ever knew what to call it.

The Man Who Doesn't Lean Forward Anymore

One of the first things that changed was physical. I didn't notice it right away. It took a while before it registered that I wasn't leaning forward in conversations anymore, literally, not metaphorically. I wasn't reaching into moments before they asked for me. I wasn't stiffening my body ahead of outcomes.

My shoulders were down. My jaw wasn't tight. My hands rested instead of hovering. Not because I put them there. They were just … there. That's the part no one tells you. Healthy masculine softness isn't something you do. It's something that happens when you stop interrupting your own nervous system.

I still showed up. I still cared. I still held lines. I just stopped crowding the moment.

FIELD NOTES
The Center

For years I thought masculinity was a straight line:

- Hard on one end, soft on the other
- Pick your lane. Whiteknuckle it. Call it "being a man."

But real life doesn't live on a line. It's a Venn diagram:

- Strength in one circle
- Softness in the other

The only place that holds—especially after divorce, especially with kids watching—is the overlap.

In that center, you can feel what's happening without becoming what's happening:
- You can stay kind without going limp
- You can hold a boundary without turning the room into a hostage situation

I used to run my presence at a ten. It was how I kept control—how I stayed ready.
Now I think of it like a dial. I don't shut it off. I adjust it.
Same man. Same values. Different volume.

Soft Eyes is the signal: I'm here. You're safe.
Strong Spine is the structure: The line still stands.

If you learned survival early, this center can feel suspicious at first.
Like if you loosen your grip, everything will fall.

But the opposite happens:

- The room gets quieter
- People stop drawing away
- And you still get to be counted on

That's what this chapter is really pointing at. Not becoming softer. Becoming steadier.

The Wall

My office is simple. Four walls. A desk. A chair. No sweeping views. Nothing designed to impress. Just a room where I work, write, read, and think—and occasionally sit still long enough to notice what's actually in my life.

The walls are cool.

They're lined with framed newspapers. Championship wins. Iconic moments. Front pages that mattered. Bruins. Red Sox. Patriots. Celtics. If you look closely, you'll even find the old Red Devils eighth-grade championship plaque from our undefeated season.

To someone else, it might look like sports nostalgia. To me, it's a map of connection.

None of it was hung to impress anyone. It wasn't curated for a visitor. There was no plan, no symmetry, no design concept. I didn't even intend to build a wall. It just happened—one frame at a time, over years.

Some I bought the morning after a win. But most arrived quietly. Gifts. Packages that showed up without announcement.

The Envelope

Mark was one of the men who taught me healthy masculinity without ever sitting me down to teach. In many ways he lived in that old-school code—loyalty, humor, and a kind of confidence that never needed to advertise itself. He also had a deep mind with broader emotional bandwidth than most.

After I moved to the Charlotte area, we kept in touch. A text now and then. Maybe seeing each other at a family event. But the real treat was anytime a Boston team made a deep run. When the city's pulse got loud again, an envelope would show up. A *Boston Globe*. From him to me. The weight of the paper inside. The smell of ink and newsprint. The headline that teleports you back north even if you're standing in a quiet kitchen down here, coffee in hand, hearing the ceiling fan hum.

This was a man that lived his professional life around manuscripts and ancient maps. Care-taking of artifacts was his business, so you can imagine the level of detail these artifacts were packed in. Total care, total precision.

I'd pull the paper out carefully, like it was something fragile. Flatten it. Smooth it. Read it like you read a letter. Each part, even the ads. And then I'd frame it. That part matters. Because framing a newspaper is ridiculous if you're just "a sports fan." But if you understand male connection and my connection to Mark, you get it.

Framing it is saying, "I received what you were really sending." Not the paper. The gesture. The loyalty. The "Ricky, I thought of you." That's healthy masculine softness in real life. Affection without performance. Connection without a speech.

The Ones That Didn't Make It

There are championships represented on that wall where the paper inside the frame is a reprint. Or a different newspaper entirely. Or a substitute that carries the moment but not the exact artifact.

The originals are gone. They were back at the old house. We tried to find them. We assumed they'd surface eventually. They never did. So when Mark passed away I replaced what I could. Not out of urgency. Not out of loss. Because it felt right.

I didn't frame the absence. I framed what remained. Some moments survive intact. Some survive altered. Some don't come with you at all. Healthy masculine softness isn't pretending that nothing was lost.

It's not needing the originals to keep going. That wall isn't complete. Neither am I. And that's okay.

A Near Miss

My journey has been mainly of awareness and progress. At times I catch the old lens coming back. A while back, I caught myself halfway through typing a long text to one of my kids. It was well-intended. It always is. Clarifying something. Making sure nothing was misunderstood. Adding context that no one had asked for.

I could feel the old wiring humming, the part of me that believes connection needs scaffolding. That silence is risky. That explanation equals care. I stopped. Deleted the draft.

Sent one clean line instead. No follow-up. No clarification. No emotional insurance policy attached. And then I let it sit. Nothing broke. That's when I knew the operating system had changed. There is a calming to presence.

The Airport Bump-In

I ran into Clark at the airport completely unplanned. We hadn't seen each other for a number of years. We both were both looking for jobs just after Covid hit, and we used to chat more often back then.

We were both waiting on coffee, half-awake, bags at our feet. After the usual catch-up, he circled back to something unfinished regarding our job hunts at the time—a moment when one of us landed on his feet and the other didn't. A stressful period for both of us. At the time it caught me off guard. I thought it was water under the bridge.

Old me would've filled the space with context: travel, work, life. Anything to smooth it over. Instead, I took a breath, trying to be honest at a time when honesty was called for, and said something like, "I didn't disappear, I just had a lot on my plate I was dealing with." He looked at me, surprised not offended. Just recalibrating. "Okay," he said. "That helps." We stood there a second longer. Not much was said for a beat, and then he found a reason to head back off to his gate.

As he walked away, he turned back. "Thanks for not bullshitting me." I watched him go and realized something else. I hadn't armored up. I hadn't collapsed. I had told the truth at the volume it belonged.

Same Hands, Different Grip

You're not a block of steel. You're layered. Strength where life pushes hardest. Flex where the people you love need gentleness. And there's another layer most men ignore—the part of you that can stay quiet long enough to read the room without tightening. Not softness. Not collapse. Calibration. It took me a long time to understand that. The right masculinity doesn't get louder. It gets better tuned.

From the outside, I doubt my kids would say anything has changed in a dramatic way. There was no announcement. No "new dad" rollout. From their side, it probably looks like this: Dad can say no without escalating. Dad can listen without solving. Dad can be quiet without disappearing. Dad can be proud without performing it. Dad can be steady without being heavy. They don't call it softness. They just feel safe.

Healthy masculine softness is not passivity. It's not checking out. It's not surrendering authority. It's not becoming agreeable or vague or undefined. It's structure without rigidity. Presence without pressure. Confidence without display. It's knowing that strength doesn't need to introduce itself.

A Small Moment
That Would Have Gotten Loud Before

I could feel the old reflex try to crank the dial back up. It happened in a parking lot, which is where a lot of real masculinity gets tested. One of the boys was late. Not catastrophically late. Just late enough that Old Eric would have started narrating the situation in his head. The internal checklist would have come online: schedule, responsibility, courtesy, the silent fear that if you don't correct this now, you're failing at something important.

I was leaning against the car, phone in my hand. He walked out, half-apologetic, half-unconcerned, the exact mix that used to light me up. Old wiring would have filled the space immediately. A comment. A joke with an edge.

A "hey, next time ..." delivered casually but carrying weight. Instead, I kept it low. I didn't say anything. I just looked at him. Soft Eyes. Neutral face. No performance. He paused just a beat longer than usual and then said, "Sorry. Lost track of time." I nodded.

"All good."

That was it. No lecture. No tone. No postgame analysis on the drive home. We got in the car and talked about something completely unrelated—music, I think—and the moment dissolved on its own. Nothing dramatic happened. Which is the point. Healthy masculine softness isn't loud. It doesn't announce itself. It doesn't need to be proven. It holds the line without tightening it. And the surprising part? The boundary landed anyway.

Soft Does Not Mean Passive

Softness isn't retreat. It isn't silence because you're afraid to speak. It isn't agreement when something inside you knows the answer is no. Healthy masculine softness still holds the line; it just doesn't become rigid while doing it. The voice stays even. The posture stays upright. The boundary stays intact.

Soft doesn't mean I won't say no. It means I won't poison the air on the way to the no. If it needs to be said, I'll say it. If it needs to be held, I'll hold it. The difference is I'm not adding heat as proof.

What disappears is the extra force, the edge, the commentary, the need to prove I'm in charge. Softness doesn't give ground. It removes friction. The kids could feel the shift. The shift showed up before anyone could explain it. Conversations got shorter, but they went deeper. Silences stopped feeling dangerous.

The room felt easier to be in. They didn't look at me to check my temperature as often. They didn't rush to manage my reaction. They didn't tighten for follow-ups. They relaxed, not because I was doing less, but because I was finally steady.

Kids don't respond to speeches. They respond to nervous systems. And when mine settled, theirs followed.

NOTES FROM A DIVORCED DAD
What to Carry Forward

- Softness doesn't mean collapse, it means access
- Strength doesn't require hardness
- Warmth is not weakness when your spine is held
- The goal isn't nicer; the goal is steadier
- Calm is a masculine skill

EMOTIONAL AVAILABILITY AT THE RIGHT FREQUENCY

Why Timing Beats Intensity

Emotional availability isn't about intensity. It's about precision. Most of us can show up. What we're learning—often later than we'd like—is how to calibrate that presence. Too much. Too flat. Too late. Being attuned isn't about frequency—it's about level. Tuning yourself before tuning to others. Healthy masculine softness is the structure. Soft Eyes, Strong Spine is the posture.

But posture alone isn't enough. You have to decide what emotional signal you're sending into the room—with your kids, your ex, your coworkers, the woman across from you at a bar, even the stranger in 14C on the flight home.

That's where this chapter lives. Not in theory. In frequency. Before we get too far into language and scales, let me show you what this looks like in the wild. It's Tuesday. Nothing cinematic.

I'm in the driveway with the engine off, phone in my hand, thumb hovering over the screen like it's a detonator.

Old wiring wants to do the thing it always does: write the whole paragraph, explain the entire context, pre-apologize for a feeling I haven't even had yet, and hit send like I'm filing a legal brief. That's 1.0 frequency. Not "bad intentions." Just too much signal. So I do the smallest thing that changes everything. I don't "think positive." I don't pep-talk myself.

I breathe once, slow enough that my shoulders drop. I soften my eyes. I feel my spine. I ask one quiet question. "What would this look like if I didn't need anything back?"

Then I take one sentence out. I send the shorter version. And the world doesn't collapse. That's the ritual. Not heroic. Repeatable. A man tuning himself before he tunes to anyone else.

FIELD NOTES
The Driveway Reset (30 Seconds)

This is the simplest one I know.
Before you text. Before you walk inside.

In the driveway, stop. One slow breath.
Let your eyes soften. Find your spine.

Quick body check: thumbs flying, jaw tight, chest
hot, stomach leaning forward—your signal is
about to come out too loud.

Ask: "Do I need anything from this person right now?"

If yes: drop one sentence, or give it **thirty seconds**.

That's it. That tiny pause is how 1.0 turns into 2.0 in real time.

There's a law of emotional physics nobody teaches boys, and few men discover on their own:

- Connection isn't built on availability; it's built on frequency
- Too low and people feel abandoned
- Too high and they feel smothered or responsible for your emotional world
- The right frequency; everything flows

The Text I Shouldn't Have Sent

Earlier in the year, before my new lens allowed me to be the person I was always meant to be, I knew my mother was coming to town for a short visit. Three nights. The kind of normal calendar thing that shouldn't mean anything more than what it is.

So I sent a simple group text to Owen, Ethan and Connor. "Could you guys come by for dinner this weekend?" Two of them said they couldn't. And here's the part that matters: Nothing was wrong yet. A grown kid saying no is not a betrayal. It's a schedule.

But my internal setting for some reason was running hot.

The fuse panel was sparking. And when you're in that state, you don't hear a neutral "no." You hear a story. Two days later, I did the thing 1.0 always did when he felt exposed. I tried to regain control with words.

I texted Owen privately a longer message, calm on the surface, loaded underneath. I told him it wasn't fair. I compared it to how fast he'd show up if his mother asked. I basically tried to teach him a lesson that was really me trying to get relief.

That's the difference between availability and frequency. I wasn't reaching for connection. I was reaching for certainty and disguising it as principle. Owen wrote back not long after. No drama. No attitude. No disappearing act.

He said he was sorry. He said he really does try. He said he thinks about fairness and splits things up as evenly as he can. Quiet. Sincere. Owen. Reading it, I felt the heat leave my chest.

Not because he "fixed it." Because I saw it. I had aimed my fog at the one kid who actually checks on my feelings. A couple days later I texted him back short. Clean. Owned. Something like "Sorry I unloaded that on you." No justification. No "but." Then I shut up.

We didn't turn it into a father-son summit. We let the repair be the repair. A month later, we did our usual retreat—me, Owen, and Connor—and it was good. Normal. Easy. We were tight the way we always are. But that earlier exchange stayed with me as a private marker because it taught me something permanent.

You can love your kids and still mistune your signal. And when you do, the move isn't to explain it prettier. The move is to own it, repair clean, and stop asking your kid to carry your pressure. Your kids love you. They always did, but they never knew which version of me they'd get— the steady, grounded Pops or the overextended dad trying to stretch a spark into a flame.

What finally changed wasn't personality. It wasn't willpower. It wasn't white-knuckle discipline. It was frequency. The moment my internal setting shifted from:

Anxious to Calm

Chasing to Steady

Overly Available to Healthily Reachable

My kids' behavior shifted almost instantly. I didn't announce it. I didn't explain it. I didn't make a speech. My nervous system just changed. And theirs relaxed.

The First Frequency Lesson: "So It's Mechanical"

It was the first time I saw someone not overreact to something breaking. Long before "emotional intelligence" was a phrase, you thought about your first lesson from a cartoon rabbit. In the old Bugs Bunny short, Bugs finally meets the dream-girl rabbit. She's perfect—ears, eyes, eyelashes. The whole scene turns romantic. Then she breaks. And a panel falls open. A metal spring shoots out.

Turns out she's a wind-up toy and not a bunny after all. Bugs, in the calmest tone imaginable, just shrugs. "So it's mechanical." He doesn't collapse. He doesn't panic. He doesn't try to fix what was never real. He simply sees what's in front of him and says, in essence, "Oh. That's what this is." Accepts the reality with brutal internal honesty for a cartoon rabbit and then moves on.

I had no idea then, but thinking back now, that was my first model of frequency neutrality. Some things fall apart. Some people reveal their wiring. Not everything is a referendum on you. Not everything needs a meltdown or a monologue. "It's mechanical" is 2.0 energy in one line.

I've always loved the ending of *The Big Lebowski* for this. The narrator watches from a distance as the Dude moves through the chaos and then eases back into his lane. He says, "I don't know about you, but I take comfort in that."

That's the whole lesson: A regulated man is oddly comforting to be around. Bugs abides, the Dude abides. Someday, you will too.

FIELD NOTES

**The Emotional Spectrum:
Where Most Men Get Stuck**

Don't think of this like a light switch, on/off.
Think dial. Volume. Thermostat.
Same words can land as calm or as pressure
depending on what your nervous system is
broadcasting underneath them.

Think of emotional frequency like a
number scale:

- 1–3 Shut down, unreadable, locked vault
- 4–5 Warm, steady, grounded
- 6–7 Open, articulate, tuned-in
- 8–10 Flooding the room, oversharing, overreacting

Most divorced dads oscillate between top and bottom ends.

Lifeless Frequency (1–3):

- Numb
- Avoidant
- Low-energy
- "I'm fine" mode
- Emotionally offline

Kids feel this as distance. So, they detach.

Over-Amplified Frequency (8–10):

- Needy texting
- Fast replies with too much emotional weight
- Emotional dumping
- Over-explaining
- Elongating every moment out of fear it will end
- Pushing for resonance, for reassurance, for more

Kids feel this as pressure. So they withdraw.

Soft Eyes, Strong Spine Frequency is the calmest path (4–7):

- Present
- Warm
- Calm
- Expecting nothing

> This is the setting your kids relax into. This is
> the signal they trust.

Greg: The Original Frequency Model

Any time he calls—any year—it's the same tone.

"Hey, man … good to hear your voice."

I learned frequency long before I had language for it. I learned it from Greg. We met in 1996. I was young, raw, still working out what kind of man I wanted to be.

The first marriage had just ended and here was Greg, also going through a divorce, and effortlessly present. He lived emotional frequency without trying. Always warm, never intrusive, always steady, never demanding.

Years could pass and then I'd call or text him. Same tone every time. No guilt. No implied "where have you been?" No emotional invoice. Just presence.

He was easy to be close to, easy to be around. No sharp edges. He's also one of the funniest humans I've ever known, but even the funny came out steady.

We lived in different states but normally got together whenever the Broncos and Patriots played—which, for some reason, felt like every year for a stretch. One Sunday in Denver, he had Pats–Broncos tickets, so I flew out and we made a weekend of it.

I met his new wife and adopted son. The new life he'd put together. A great weekend, like always with Greg. No agendas. All good.

On the way to the stadium, we swung past his buddy's house

to grab the tickets. We stood in the doorway talking, and Greg mentioned—casual, like it was nothing—that his friend was "trying to take it easy."

A few weeks earlier the guy had gotten the call from his doctor. All the wrong numbers were up. Need to get salt down. Drinking down. The whole adult-scolding.

Two hours later, we found the tailgate by instinct. Grills going. Beers flowing. A sea of orange and navy. Greg is already laughing with a group. He's found the buddy. The newly responsible one. The guy immediately shows Greg where the beers are.

I spot him nearby. Cigarette hanging out of his mouth. Big smile. Plate piled high with sausage and anything salty and fatty within reach.

Greg comes back with a beer for me. Same half-grin. He nods toward another guy in the circle and cracking up, he says, "That's his doctor." Not just any doctor. *His doctor.* The guy who gave the speech about salt and sugar is standing there with a beer in his hand, apparently off duty.

Greg is laughing. No panic. No awkwardness. No drama. Just Greg, right on time. That was the blueprint. I just wasn't tuned to it yet.

FIELD NOTES
The Composite Antenna

I've spent decades selling composite materials for aircraft.

So here's a metaphor I can't unsee:

- A great composite part isn't one solid hunk of steel
- It's layers: different fibers, different orientations, different resins
- Perhaps even a conductive layer or an antenna element right into the structure so the part can receive, transmit, or sense what's happening around it

That's healthy masculinity, too. Not a monolith. A layup.

- Structure where life will push hardest
- Flex where the people you love need softness and a tuned "antenna"
- If your masculinity is "always hard" or "always shut down," it's brittle.

If it's "always emotional," it's noisy.

The right frequency is elegantly engineered.

Why Frequency Matters More Than Words

The older you get, the more obvious this becomes. Humans respond less to language and more to nervous systems. Here's how you know this is real: People feel it before you say a word. I wrote some of this chapter after a normal run to CVS, one of those "I'm just going to grab a few things" trips that turns into you standing in the pharmacy lane having a tiny human interaction you didn't schedule.

A woman with tired eyes, dealing with her own list, looks at the line, and you can tell she's annoyed. She moves away, then doubles back and leans into my space like we're coworkers for a second and says, quietly, "I just talked to him, the computer is resetting. You may want to shop and come back. I may just wait."

And I casually let her know, no rush here, "I'll wait it out with you. Thanks." That's it. No number exchange. No story. No "my life is complicated." Just two humans crossing paths with the right signal strength. If I'm broadcasting 8–10, that moment doesn't happen. If I'm broadcasting 1–3, I don't even notice it.

But on a good 2.0 day—Soft Eyes, Strong Spine—life hands you these little micro-connections like proof. Not because of you. Because you're not leaking need into the room.

That's frequency. People don't need "the right words." They need the right setting. They read your breath, your pacing, your tone, the warmth in your eyes, your posture, the speed of your reactions.

Your kids feel it even more. You can say "I'm not mad" in a voice that makes their stomach drop. You can say almost nothing and have them feel completely safe. When your frequency is right, they don't need explanations.

Their bodies simply go, "I feel good around Dad." Everything else is commentary. Less draining, more magnetic.

Most men try to become more interesting. The real magic is becoming less draining. When people don't lose energy around you, they finally have energy for you. That's what 2.0 frequency does. It stops pulling on everyone in the room so connection can finally happen on its own.

The silent evidence: how my kids respond now. When the frequency started shifting, I didn't explain myself or label it. Simply started living Soft Eyes, Strong Spine. And they felt it.

Owen's humor came back clean, unburdened. Connor's newfound use of "Pops" slid out with zero tension. Anna answered a couple basic texts with possible warmth after nine years of drift. And Ethan's response was the quietest and somehow the most profound. His texts didn't suddenly get longer or deeper. They got lighter. Effortless. Unweighted.

A six-word message that used to read like careful distance suddenly carried ease. A meme here. A one-liner there. A small laugh in the digital space between father and son. He didn't need repair. He didn't need emotional surgery. He didn't need an apology tour to reopen a channel that had never fully closed. He just needed steadiness.

Ethan is the living proof that when a man stops broadcasting too hot or too cold, the kids who were already loosely secure don't suddenly gush, they simply relax. I didn't force closeness. I created space. And in that space, they came toward me. That's emotional availability at the right frequency: "I'm here. I love you. You owe me nothing."

The Visit You Didn't Overplan

Before clarity started to set in, a senior-year fall with Owen would have been treated like a countdown clock. Staring at the calendar, feeling the sand running out.

2.0 frequency moves differently. One ordinary week in October, I just texted, "Hey, how about I come out Sunday and we watch football?" No speech. No pressure. Just a signal: I'd like to be with you.

The timing worked out well, so I drove to Myrtle Beach. I met him at his apartment near campus. I saw his life instead of staging an event. I threw a football with his roommate. I ran to the grocery store for game-day food. We fished a little. We watched the games.

I didn't stretch the day into something it didn't want to be. I didn't overstay or push for a big dinner. I used my Marriott points, grabbed a hotel, and the next morning I simply drove back home. No grand exit. No "remember this, son" speech. Just ease.

A few days later I mailed a small care package. A quiet, dad-level reinforcement of the life he was building. Long-sleeve polyester fishing shirts, some bug spray for the mosquitoes, and a couple of practical odds and ends. He was working in the heat of late Carolina summer, field work on a Marine Biology project, helping write a paper about the way marshes absorb carbon. I didn't make it a big moral lesson. I just sent the gear. And then, weeks later, this showed up on my phone: "Out doing field work in the new shirt my father got me."

Steady presence pays off quietly.

The Text That Told Me My Frequency Landed

Every dad wants a scoreboard. Most of us pretend we don't. Sometimes you get one, and it doesn't arrive as a trophy. It comes as a message from your son that makes you sit down.

I've mentioned some of Owen's texts along this journey and my text that almost sabotaged the bond. Owen sent me a text in the heat of my awakening that started with a line that basically said "We don't talk too serious, but I've been thinking."

Then he did what grown sons almost never do in plain language—he told me he felt blessed I was his father. That he still quotes my "Dadisms," that those old car rides and ordinary rituals stayed in him.

I'm not putting it here as a flex. I'm putting it here as a measurement. Because kids don't praise your speeches. They praise your signal. When a son says, "I quote you," what he's really saying is:

"Your frequency built something in me that still holds."

The text itself was simple font. No heart emoji. No photo to punctuate the message. Just a son, waist-deep in his own emerging life, pausing long enough to say, "I feel you here with me."

That's frequency. Not hovering. Not absent. Present at the right signal strength—enough to be felt, not so much he had to manage you.

Availability without need. Not instant replies.

Not being on call 24/7. Not bleeding your anxiety onto your kids by narrating every feeling in real time.

It's this: "I'm reachable. I'm responsive. I'm not asking you to carry me." 2.0 emotional availability means you can be interrupted. You can hear hard things. You can talk about your life at an intensity they can handle. You don't use them as your therapist. You don't make your storms their problem. Soft Eyes without a Strong Spine turns into approval-seeking.

Connor feels that now. Owen feels it in the marsh. Ethan feels it in how I handle the relationship. Anna feels it in the way I didn't flood her when she cracked the door.

The frequency says, "You never have to manage my feelings to keep me." That is the core of non-needy fatherhood.

FIELD NOTES
The 3-Second Frequency Test

Here is one clean question you can ask anytime:

- "If my kid got this version of me for the next ten minutes, would they relax or tighten?"

Don't overthink it. Your body will answer before your brain.

- If the answer is "relax," you're in the 4–7 band.
- If the answer is "tighten," that's 8–10 or 1–3 territory.

Then do a tiny adjustment: "One notch toward steady."
Not perfect. Not enlightened. Just a little more calm, a little less performance.

How Women Feel Frequency

This isn't a "how to get women" section. This is about signal—because women tend to read it faster than men do. Not because they're magical. Because they've had to. Most women have spent a lifetime tracking men's moods for safety, for sanity, for timing. They feel your nervous system before they hear your words.

So when you start living at a steadier frequency, women notice. The clerk at the hotel desk notices. The stranger in 14C notices. Not because you're performing calm—because you actually are calm.

Same ranges as before. This time it's emotional volume—the way you come into a room. Too loud feels unsafe. Too dead feels unsafe. Steady feels like you can be trusted with real life.

- A man broadcasting at 8–10 (Over-Amplified) reads as overwhelming, needy, high-maintenance, emotionally unsafe
- A man broadcasting at 1–3 (Lifeless) reads as rigid, distant, unavailable, uninterested
- A man at 4–7 (2.0 Frequency) feels like safety, maturity, clear edges but open heart, someone who can handle complexity without making it all about him

That's why the CVS micro-moment mattered. She responded before I "did" anything. Not to words. To my nervous system.

A steady man who isn't hunting is rare.

That's not a throwaway line. Check it with a woman you trust. You won't need to explain what you mean. A man who isn't scanning, chasing, or trying to extract something feels safe. And safety is where connection starts.

Understanding frequency changes everything. How strangers feel you. How women sense you. How coworkers trust you. How you talk. How you text. How you breathe. Once you understand emotional frequency, you start to notice another quiet truth about men.

We don't just feel in bursts. We often think in bursts. We read in short runs, scroll in loops, come back to the same paragraph five times before it "lands." Not because we're shallow, but because our minds are tracking a dozen threats and responsibilities in the background.

There's a cognitive layer underneath all this—the mental bandwidth that makes my new frequency possible. The ability to focus. To absorb. To read deeply. To stay. To not run from your own life. And it leads to a quietly revealing truth about myself—and about a lot of other men: We read in bursts, and that pattern says something real about the man I was and the man I've become.

NOTES FROM A DIVORCED DAD
What to Carry Forward

- Availability without attunement can still miss the moment
- Frequency matters more than volume
- "Right" isn't constant, it's responsive
- Presence is felt before it's understood
- When you tune correctly, connection costs less

WHY CALM MEN BECOME MAGNETIC

When Frequency Changes Everything

Becoming magnetic is what happens when a man stops broadcasting need, threat, or performance—and starts broadcasting steadiness. Women notice that. Your kids feel it even more.

You can tell a lot about a man by watching him in an airport. Not the version smiling for the gate agent. Not the version making polite small talk at the coffee kiosk. The real version. The one who's half-awake, suspended between where he came from and where he's going.

It's in these in-between spaces that a man's nervous system tells the truth. Some men move like they're being hunted. Some men move like they're in a fog, their bodies present but their minds two states ahead.

And then, once in a while, you see a man who moves differently.

Not fast. Not slow. Just ... settled. His presence unhurried. For most of my life, I wasn't that man.

I was the one doing mental math on flight times, unread emails, conversations that hadn't happened yet. I was physically in the terminal but mentally already landing, already solving, already managing. That's Eric 1.0. A man always slightly ahead of his actual life. 2.0 is the moment he finally catches up.

The last chapter explained tuning your emotional signal. This chapter shows what happens when that signal actually stabilizes inside your body and turns a man into someone people can breath easier near without knowing why.

To understand why calm men become magnetic, we start not in a terminal but across the street from my house in Gastonia.

The Soft Glow Across the Street

I like the airport in the morning. I'll get up stupid early for the first flight just to have the world to myself for a while. The quiet before the day crowds in. The feeling that I'm slipping out ahead of the noise.

That morning the street was still—cool air, no movement. From the driveway I could see the Christmas lights I'd hung that weekend: a simple line along the porch and four flickering candle lights in the front windows. Soft. Steady. They landed in the darkness just right.

A month earlier, my new neighbor—mid-forties, warm eyes, a life written softly in her face—had offered a brief hello. In the old version of me, a moment like that never stayed small. My mind would start working it, stretching it forward, looking for a way in.

I could've looked at those window candles and thought, *Maybe she'll notice. Maybe it gives me an opening.* A reason to flirt. A way to turn a decent moment into a move. None of it real—just me trying to manufacture something that didn't need to be made.

But that morning my mind didn't go there.

My window glowed gently. Not bright. Not demanding. Just lived-in. And my first thought wasn't a strategy or a storyline. No projection. No what-if movie trailer. Just presence.

There was a small, real connection in that moment—even without her there. Not the familiar masculine surge of winning or momentum but something steadier. A warmth that didn't ask for anything. It felt right. It felt good. It felt complete.

What I once would have labeled feminine—the stillness, the resonance, the capacity to let something be enough—wasn't feminine at all. It was calm. And standing there in the early morning, holding another person in mind, I realized how rare it had been for me to feel that calm while staying fully at home in myself.

The Airport Linger

I was becoming more aware of changes to myself and my vibe. I was back in an airport and just standing near the line of people waiting for coffee. Not doing anything important.

People moved past me like currents splitting around a stone. That's when I felt her presence before I even saw her. Dark hair. Clean outfit. A kind of poised tiredness. She hovered near me. Not close, but close enough to feel like an echo.

When I stepped out, she stepped out. When I paused by the coffee stand, she paused. The old version of me would've immediately started building meaning out of proximity. *Is she interested? Is this a sign? Should I do something? Should I say something? What's the move?*

1.0 would have built an entire future based on proximity. But 2.0 me saw something else entirely. She wasn't responding to my face. Or my words. Or my outfit. She was responding to the calm in my body. My pacing. My breathing. My unhurried eyes. My absence of internal static.

Calm isn't neutral. Calm is atmospheric. Because I wasn't reaching toward her, she drifted toward me. Women feel your nervous system before they hear your words.

Rapp and Reacher, What a Combo

Earlier I mentioned men and how we read in bursts. I was never a big reader, but for about ten years—before phones turned into minicomputers—travel gave me long stretches with nothing to do but read.

I wasn't the man with a stack on the nightstand and a highlighter. I was the man who bought a book in an airport like he was buying a tool. I'd walk into that little bookstore at the end of the concourse and my hand would go straight to the same shelf: Jack Reacher. Mitch Rapp.

Men who don't explain. Men who don't audition. Men who don't beg the room to agree with them. I wasn't reading to escape. I was reading to borrow a nervous system. Reacher doesn't rush. Rapp doesn't flinch.

They move like the world is loud, and they're not obligated to match it. And that calm—fictional, printed, cheap paper and glue—still did something real inside me. The funny part is I didn't know that's what I was doing. I thought I just liked action. I thought I had an "attention-span problem."

But the truth is, my mind didn't want long, quiet middles. It wanted edges. Starts. Stops. Stakes. Airports are basically a shrine to scan mode. Screens. Gate changes. Announcements. A hundred little reasons to sprint internally. So I'd read in bursts. Ten pages. Twenty. Put it down. Pick it up. Put it down again.

Not because the story wasn't good. I'd read a few pages, then stop. Stillness felt like taking my hand off the wheel—like letting the world move without me for a moment.

Why Calm Men Become Magnetic

A calm man sends one unmistakable, unspoken message. "I'm not a burden. I'm not a threat. I'm not asking you to carry me." Most men don't realize how often they broadcast the opposite.

They walk into rooms as problems. They project need. They radiate tension. Even when they're "nice," there's an undercurrent of wanting something. Validation. Attention. Control. A win. And people feel that. They feel it as a drain.

Calm is the opposite. Calm enlarges the room. Calm is breathable.

Kids feel this. Women feel this. Coworkers feel this. Strangers feel this from across a concourse. Calm isn't impressive. Calm is livable.

FIELD NOTES
Less Draining, More Magnetic

Most men work hard to be interesting.
What actually changes relationships is being
easier to be around.
When people don't lose energy around you, they
have energy for you.

Publix, the Grocery Store Lab

I used to think being magnetic was some mysterious charisma thing. Something you're born with, or you're not. Now I think it's simpler and almost annoyingly practical.

Calm men become magnetic because people can feel they're not going to be managed. The funny part is that you don't have to test this in some high-stakes environment. You can test it in the most normal place on earth—a grocery store.

I went to Publix on one of those days where I was just trying to be a grown man. Eat a little better. Swap out the big five-gallon water jugs. Grab a rotisserie chicken instead of fried for dinner. And I started noticing what I used to miss because 1.0 me never truly arrived anywhere.

The small interactions. The micro-signals. The human-to-human exchanges that happen when you're not sprinting through life like a man trying to outrun his own thoughts.

First was Mustache Man. Late-sixties, kind face, round in that "life happened" way. We passed near the water exchange, and he gave me a nod that was a little more than a nod. A soft smile that said: "I see you." No words. No performance. Just that half-second of mutual recognition.

In 1.0, that moment wouldn't have landed. I would've already been thinking about the next aisle, the next task, the next email, the next thing. In 2.0, it landed. And it didn't need to become anything bigger than what it was.

Then the bakery hellos. Not loud. Not performative. Just there. The kind of Southern friendliness that still catches my Northeast reflexes off guard—not because it's excessive, but because it's unguarded. Eye contact. A pause. Someone actually waiting for your answer.

It's small, but I notice it now. The way people stay with you for half a second longer than required. The way the interaction isn't rushed to completion. Nothing is being sold, extracted, or managed. It's just a brief moment of shared presence before the day moves on.

And then there was Rotisserie Chicken Lady. She had that delivery-run look—you could tell. Late-forties, no-nonsense, just real. She was pissed because the chickens in the case were all weird flavors: peach hot, mango jerk. Stuff that sounded like a cocktail menu, not dinner. She asked the guy behind the counter if there was any "regular" chicken, then drifted off, irritated. I stepped up and thought: *Screw it. How bad can peach hot chicken be?* I grabbed it.

And as I'm lowering it into my cart, she steps back into my space—quiet, almost conspiratorial—like we're two undercover agents in the poultry aisle. "I just talked to him," she says. "He's gonna bring out more regular chicken. I don't know what that flavor is."

And I smiled. Not in a flirty way. Not in a "thanks, sweetheart" way. Just a human way. "Me either," I said. "But I'm gonna give it a shot anyway. Thanks though." And that was the whole thing. A small kindness offered. A small kindness received. No hook. No story. No "oh, maybe this is a chance to meet." Just two people in a grocery store, keeping the world slightly less harsh for ten seconds. That's 2.0.

The next one was the stock girl. Mid-twenties, tattooed, moving fast. As I passed, there was a brief moment of eye contact—direct, neutral. Soft eyes. Strong spine. She clocked me.

That surprised me. Not because it meant anything, but because 1.0 would have been invisible. Rushed. Unreadable. 2.0 registered. Not interesting. Not uninteresting. Just present. No story. No spiral. I noticed it and kept shopping.

Then came Tired Old Divorced Lady at the register. Late-sixties. Northern transplant. That polite-but-bitter energy of someone who never expected to be bagging groceries at this age. I've seen her before, but that day she was extra chatty. And I could feel her trying to find "an appropriate topic."

Like she wanted to connect but didn't want to risk being weird. I had bought a new dish mat because apparently that's what your life becomes at fifty-seven. You get excited about a dish mat like it's a new set of rims. She commented on it and then kind of stammered, like she wasn't sure where to take it. So I gave her a soft landing.

"Yeah," I said, "I had my old one for years. Finally decided it was time." That's it. No big speech. No over-helping. No "tell me your life story." And she lit up just a little, like she'd been given permission to be normal again.

She told me to have a wonderful Thanksgiving. I told her the same. And I walked away feeling something that 1.0 me didn't understand—connection doesn't have to be deep to be real.

Last stop was Lottery Lady. It was my birthday, so I decided to do something that made me think of Tom. He played the lottery every day. He always claimed he didn't but after the accident we found a box of old tickets in his trunk. Classic Tom.

So I'm standing there filling out the slip, and I realize I only ever play the big ones. Mega Millions. Powerball. I never mess with the Pick 3/Pick 4 stuff. Not since moving south. Not since I started noticing how many people treat the lottery counter like church.

I bring my slip to Lottery Lady and tell her I want Mega Millions and Powerball, and then I point at the other stuff like a rookie. "I've never played these before." She looks at me and asks, "Are you from New York?"

"No," I said. "Boston." And she smiles—not a polite retail smile. She gives me an "ohhhh, okay, that makes sense" smile. Then she does something that feels so small but is actually the whole point of this chapter. She helps me. Not because I demanded it. Not because I performed. Not because I flirted. Just because my signal said: "I'm here, I'm normal, I'm not a threat, and I'm not asking you to carry me."

She grabs an eraser and starts fixing my slip like a seasoned bookmaker, explaining box versus straight the way someone explains how to turn a screwdriver. I can tell she's a little bit of a gambler. A little bit of a survivor. Early sixties. Firm build. Grey streaks. A hard-life grin.

And none of it is a turn-on or a turn-off. It's not even in that category. It's just … real.

She asks how long I've been here. I start doing the math

in my head and say, "Almost twenty years." Then I add, "Actually … eighteen. Just before my youngest was born." Without meaning to, I hit her with kryptonite.

Something in her shifts. She leans in a little, like the conversation just got easier.

She starts telling me about her cat. She wanted to name it Cam Neely, but her granddaughter wanted something else, so they named it Stanley and called it Stan.

And I'm laughing, trying to pull away, and she's trying to pull me in with one more story, one more detail, one more moment. Finally I do what calm men do. I end it cleanly. "Ha," I said. "I'll see you around." And I walked out with my lottery ticket and my peach hot chicken and a quiet, slightly absurd sense that I had just watched my whole thesis play out in the aisles of the Publix.

Here's the part that matters. None of those people were responding to what "magnetic" actually is. Not game. Not lines. Not smooth talk.

It's a man whose body isn't broadcasting "please fix me." It's broadcasting "I'm good. I'm here. Relax near me." That's the whole thing. And once you see it in Publix, you start seeing it everywhere.

In Publix I could see the effect. But the deeper question is why is it so rare? Why do so many men feel like they're running even when they're standing still? It's not because they're broken men. It's because their systems were trained for a different job.

When life teaches you to be useful, you become a scanner. You read faces. You read rooms. You read the weather in a voice. You preload the next move so nobody catches you flat-footed. It looks like competence. It is competence. It's also exhausting.

Scan mode is great for survival and spreadsheets. It's terrible for intimacy. Because you can't be magnetic when your body is broadcasting one message: Something is about to go wrong and I'm the one who has to handle it.

Calm isn't "chill." Calm is when your body finally stops acting like the future is an emergency. Calm is anchor mode—the ability to drop your weight into the moment without losing yourself.

FIELD NOTES
Scan Mode vs. Anchor Mode

Scan Mode (Eric 1.0)

- Preloading: running the next three steps before the current one is done
- Pattern-recognition: catching the shift in someone's tone before they admit it
- Micro-observation: watching hands, eyes, exits, threats, opportunities
- Tactical time: every minute has a job
- High signal/low noise: short, dense, efficient

Anchored Mode (Eric 2.0)

- Letting the moment hold the frame
- Staying with what's actually happening—not what might happen
- Stillness that doesn't feel like danger
- Full breaths, full sentences, full attention

> - A body that says: "I can handle life without
>   sprinting"
>
> If you grew up around tension, grounded mode
> can feel like vulnerability.
> If you grew up around chaos, quiet can feel like
> the calm before the hit.
> So you keep scanning. You keep moving. You
> keep "being a man."
> But the magnet isn't the hustle. The magnet is
> the steadiness underneath it.

AutoZone—The Battery Store Lab

A few weeks after Publix, I got another reminder that calm shows up in the normal places of life. Connor's car battery finally died—the original one, the kind you forget is old until it quits on a cold morning. He had school and life to get to, so we swapped cars. He took mine, and I took his car.

Before handing over the keys, he'd borrowed his mom's portable charger and left it in the trunk, just in case. He'd already tried it twice—enough to get the car turned over and moved to where it needed to be. Responsible in a quiet way. It wasn't something I asked for. It just showed up. Maybe that's what the frequency shift looks like.

I went to the AutoZone next to the Planet Fitness and got helped by a friendly man—easy, unhurried, country without the act. Calm, meticulous. Old me would've been three steps ahead of him in my mind, trying to compress the moment into fifteen seconds.

I gave the man my number so he could look it up in the system. I said it fast, like an operator—three digits at a time. Too fast. We backed it down to one digit at a time. "Seven." "Zero." "Four." Slow, deliberate. The pace I wouldn't have chosen.

Halfway through, a guy walked in—mid-thirties—and they traded the Southern "hey." The man behind the counter had what I've learned to recognize as Soft Eyes. When the younger guy asked how he was doing, he said, without drama, "I'm doin' it for an ol' guy."

When we finished, he looked at the screen and said it plainly: My number wasn't in the system.

That used to be the kind of friction that lit me up—proof, in my body, that I needed to take over. 1.0 me would've leaned forward, ready to prove I belonged in the database. Ready to make it a thing.

Instead, I felt the moment for what it was: not my arena. Not worth my emotional energy. I met his eyes and just told the truth.

"Yeah," I said. "I've moved a lot." We got it sorted. My card threw a little "alert cashier" message and I made one dry joke— nothing performative, just a small release—and he gave me that look that said he'd heard it all and didn't mind hearing it again.

The buying was quick. The install took longer. He had a bum hand, so I hauled out the old battery for him and we talked while we worked.

What I remember isn't the battery. It's that I didn't feel rushed. I didn't try to take control of a process that wasn't mine. I let the pace be the pace, and it didn't cost me anything. If anything, it gave something back—a micro-connection with a man a decade or two older, out there on a cold day doing his job with presence. A small pivot point. Not because the world changed. Because I did.

That's the part men miss when they chase "magnetic." They think it's about pulling people in. It's not. It's about being steady enough that you don't poison the air over a minor inconvenience. He finished. Wiped his hands. Gave me the simplest nod done. And I drove away thinking: *How many of your days were built out of little urges to sprint?*

FIELD NOTES
Why Men Think and Love in Bursts

Men think in bursts because bursts feel like control.

Intensity lets us outrun discomfort.

Urgency feels like purpose.

Projection feels safer than presence.

Closure feels safer than staying open.

Calm stretches the bursts into something human.

A calm man listens fully, stays seated inside himself, and stops rehearsing responses, stops clenching moments, loves without securing the future.

Calm doesn't eliminate the bursts. It gives them room to breathe.

Life in Practice

There's a strange moment that happens after you have your awakening. A moment where you realize, Okay, I'm different. I can see myself. I can feel the shift. Now what? Awakening is not the finish line. It's the ignition.

The hard part comes next, when life doesn't test you with crises but with ordinary Tuesday mornings. When no one is watching. When the kids are snippy. When the house is messy. When your ex sends a text that could easily pull you back into your old pattern. When your body wants to default to urgency.

This part is different. This is where the work becomes practice. Not the kind of practice you post about. The kind of practice you live. The kind that builds a calm life out of boring days, Dadisms, and the small, strange moments your kids never forget.

Practice is fatherhood lived quietly, without coiling. Practice is masculinity without noise. Practice is saying no without defensiveness. Practice is staying seated inside yourself even when the room starts to heat up. Practice is choosing the signal you want to broadcast over the reflex you were trained to obey.

If the first half of the book was the climb out of the old life, this is the part where we build the new one. The days when it feels like art, and the days when it feels like a lost signal.

Life in practice is where Soft Eyes, Strong Spine becomes real. Where frequency becomes behavior. Where we stop talking about becoming the man and start being him.

NOTES FROM A DIVORCED DAD
What to Carry Forward

- Calm creates gravity, no chasing required
- Stability invites trust without explanation
- A regulated man becomes a place people can land
- Confidence is quieter than performance
- The magnet isn't charisma. It's steadiness.

PART IV

LIFE IN PRACTICE

What Gets Passed Down

Here is where the ideas stop being ideas. Practice is what carries them forward. Quietly. Repeatedly. This is where posture turns into pattern, and pattern turns into something your kids can rely on without ever naming.

There are no speeches here. No heroic moments. Just small, consistent signals—how you enter a room, how you hold a line, how you stay present without pressing. The kind of steadiness children don't analyze but feel immediately. The kind that lowers the temperature without asking for credit.

This is how values actually get passed down. Not as lessons but as lived codes. The way a goodbye feels. The way conflict settles instead of escalating. The way your presence says, "You're safe here," even when nothing is being explained.

Over time, those moments stack. They become memory. Then expectation. Then inheritance. This is where Soft Eyes, Strong Spine stops being a concept and starts becoming something your kids carry forward—long after they forget how it began.

THE CODES MEN PASS DOWN

What Men Carry Forward

By now, you've seen the pattern. 2.0 is a hundred small moves—tiny, almost invisible choices that change your nervous system first so your behavior can follow. Every man thinks he'll be defined by the big moments—the speeches, the wins, the perfect days.

But the truth is simpler, quieter, older. A man is revealed by his rituals. His systems. His codes. His private ways of creating order in a world built to tip us off balance. This chapter is about those codes, the ones you lived long before you ever knew their names.

The Lobster Ritual

A man's deepest wiring doesn't show up in grand moments. It shows up in the tiny rituals no one else notices. For some men it's mowing the lawn in perfect diagonal lines. For others it's sharpening every knife before cooking. For others it's the same booth, same breakfast, same exact seat at the bar. For me? It was lobster. Not eating it, engineering it.

Every piece cracked. Every shell removed. Every knuckle cleaned out. Every tail sliced. Every membrane gone. A perfect mound of ready-to-eat lobster piled neatly on the plate. Only then would I take the first bite.

When I was eight, people laughed. When I was thirty, people joked. When I was forty, people rolled their eyes with affection. But none of them realized the truth. This was never about lobster.

This was my first language. The blueprint. The nervous system. The architecture of who I was becoming: a man who removes the chaos before he enters the moment.

The Lobster Strategy Explained

I wasn't cracking claws, I was clearing space. I wasn't being particular, I was preparing for clarity. I wasn't delaying comfort, I was building calm. I've always been this man.

Version 2.0 didn't change who I am. It revealed what was already there. The pattern now shows up everywhere by reducing noise so people can breathe. Clearing emotional debris so that connection can begin. Showing a steadiness that lets my boys find their footing.

The way strangers are settling near me and women are softening around me. The way my presence organizes a room. The way my frequency tells people they're safe.

I have always been a man who makes order so others can rest. A man who prepares the internal landscape before anyone else arrives. What I have learned is: That's the real lobster strategy. Create peace so connection has somewhere to land.

FIELD NOTES
"Lobster Men" vs. "Chaos Men"

There are two types of men.

Chaos Men dive straight in. They react fast, skip preparation, and leave emotional clutter everywhere. Things work—until someone has to clean up after the moment.

Lobster Men prepare first. They eliminate friction and keep the environment clean so others can relax and savor what's happening.

I was a Lobster Man before I ever had words for it.

The Book as a Lobster Ritual

Those first lobsters were at McMenemy's Seafood in Brockton for the Friday night double lobster special. Claws, knuckles, tail. I cracked every piece before tasting a thing. Not to show off, not because someone taught it that way. I did it to settle myself.

That was the first moment my nervous system said, "If I clear the chaos, I can finally enjoy what's in front of me." I've lived that code ever since and naming it allows me to see the reserved simplicity in the move.

I didn't know it at the time, but the lobster ritual is the same way I've been writing this book. Not the romantic part, not the parts where the sentences land and the chapters suddenly feel alive. The part before that. The part that looks like nothing from the outside.

Writing a book isn't one clean sit-down where wisdom shows up on schedule. It's more like cracking lobster—messy, unglamorous, requiring patience, and weirdly satisfying when you finally clear the noise.

There's the part people see—chapters, pages, a clean sentence that lands. And then there's the part nobody sees: the steady, repetitive work of making order out of your own mind without getting dramatic about it.

This was the surprise for me: The book didn't get better when I got "inspired." It got better when I showed up like a grown man—calm, consistent, not hunting for a mood. Same way you don't crack the first claw with adrenaline. You crack it with sequence.

Every meaningful thing has a broccoli phase, the unglamorous prep you do so you can enjoy what you're building without gagging on the chaos. Some men treat broccoli like punishment. Prepared men treat it like fuel. They don't need to call it discipline. They just do it.

Steady Man Code: Respect Sequence

Most men try to skip to the feast. Steady men respect sequence. They know the order matters. They know what happens when you try to enjoy something you haven't prepared for: You don't actually enjoy it; you manage it. And managing is the old life. That's why this part of the book begins here. Because everything in Part IV is practice, and practice requires a framework.

The lobster ritual looks like a food thing, but what it really is and always has been is a container. I created steadiness before I touched the meal. I removed friction before I asked myself to be present.

That's why people loved being around me during those dinners, even if they couldn't name why. It wasn't the lobster. It was the absence of drama. My nervous system wasn't searching for the next problem. It had already handled the problems. That's what 2.0 feels like when it's real: not "better behavior" but less interference.

Preparation isn't the calendar. It's the body. You know you're prepared when you stop arguing with the work. When your shoulders drop. When you're not checking your phone every thirty seconds to escape your own discomfort. When you can sit in the task without narrating it, defending it, or resenting it. That's the moment the ritual is doing what rituals are supposed to do: It's telling the nervous system, "You're safe. You can proceed."

This code doesn't stay in the kitchen. It begins to show up everywhere. It shows up in how you drive with your kids in the car—steady, not frantic. It shows up in how you send a text—clean, not performative. It shows up in how you walk into a room—not scanning for who needs managing.

You start creating peace instead of chasing it. And you start noticing that other people can feel it before you say a word. That's why the lobster ritual is quietly one of the most important scenes in the whole book. It's a living example of Soft Eyes, Strong Spine without the speech. It shows up on a Tuesday afternoon when your phone lights up and the old wiring wakes up with it.

In 1.0, you would have treated that screen like a courtroom. You'd start building the case before the other person ever replied. One long message, then another. A "just making sure" that wasn't actually making sure of anything. Your thumbs would sprint. You'd feel the heat rise and still call it "communication."

The new lens does something boring and powerful: You crack the shells first. You type the first draft—the one with the edge in it—and you delete it. You set the phone down. You take a few slow breaths while the dishwater runs. You let your shoulders drop.

Then you send one clean line that doesn't carry heat, because you're not carrying heat. "Pickup at six. I'll have them ready."

Your kids may never remember a specific lobster dinner the way you remember it. They don't have to. What they remember is the air around you. A dad who wasn't rushed. A dad who didn't snap over small friction. A dad who could handle a complicated moment without turning it into a crisis.

That's how codes get passed down in real families. Not through lectures. Through repetition. Public calm can be performance. Private calm becomes character.

The real practice happens when no one is clapping. When you're alone with the work. When you're cracking shells because that's the way you are, not because someone is watching. And the wild part is your kids can feel that practice even when they never see it. Because what you practice in private becomes the man they grow up around. That's inheritance.

Set Yourself Up to Win

Most men think growth requires willpower. They believe lines like: *Pain is weakness leaving the body. Stare down the trigger. Out-discipline the old version of yourself.* But anyone who's ever lived in 1.0 knows the truth. When your environment is rigged against you, you'll lose even on your best days.

When your environment is rigged for you, you don't need "willpower" at all. That was one of the quiet breakthroughs of my 2.0 shift. I stopped trying to wrestle my nervous system into submission and started building rooms I could breathe in. Not perfect rooms. Not rooms meant to impress. Just simple, repeatable, micro-designed setups that nudged me toward the calm, steady version of myself that me and my kids needed.

I didn't change my soul. I changed the settings. Here's how: First, I change what I see. I learn something simple but powerful: My brain believes the room I'm in. So I change my phone wallpaper to something grounding instead of something emotional. I swap out an avatar that carries weight for one that carries ease. I even change how I light the living room—lamps on, overheads off—because 2.0 doesn't do floodlights.

These aren't aesthetic choices. They're nervous-system cues. When the visuals are calm, you get calm. When the visuals are chaotic, old patterns rush back. This was the first rule of 2.0: Set the stage so you don't have to fight the scene. Set yourself up to win. Clear the simple paths so the complex ones can be worked on later.

Second, you changed where you stand. You started noticing that certain places brought out your worst impulses. The wrong aisle at the gym. The TV showing cable news. The treadmill next to the guy who grunts like he's in labor. The family gathering where everyone sits in the same chairs they've sat in since 1992.

So you started doing what calm men do: You put yourself in cleaner lanes. A different TV. A better time slot. A treadmill that lets you face away from the noise. A seat at the table that didn't put you in the emotional splash zone. Small shifts. Massive difference. Instead of reactive mode, you moved into receiving mode, which is exactly where Soft Eyes and a Strong Spine live.

Third, you built micro-rituals. Your brain responded beautifully to silent agreements with yourself. Not resolutions. Not "I swear I'll never do X again." Just anchors, tiny rituals that told your body, "We're safe. We know how this goes." The same shorts, sweat towel, and zip-up for the gym, your "Dude abides" uniform. The same playlist before a hard day. The same water bottle in the same cup holder on the same drive.

The same morning rhythm on travel days. These weren't compulsions. They were stability cues. Micro-systems don't have to be deep. They just have to be repeatable. And the real magic? They cut your emotional reactivity in half. When the ritual held, you held.

Fourth, you designed out the triggers. You stopped expecting yourself to be a Navy SEAL of emotional fortitude. Instead, you became a carpenter quietly removing the tripwires in the room. You muted group chats that pulled you off balance. You rearranged your apps. You unfollowed accounts that weaponized comparison. You organized your kitchen and living room in a way that felt breathable, not scattered.

The principle was the same: Don't hope you'll be regulated later. Set things up so you don't get dysregulated in the first place. It's a lot easier to avoid a landslide than to dig yourself out of one.

Fifth, you made 2.0 the default setting (not the performance). This is the final piece, the one most divorced dads never unlock. 2.0 didn't become "special mode." It became your background mode, your always-on mode.

The micro-systems made that possible. Because instead of waking up each day trying to "hold it together," you woke up each day already held by the environment you built—cleaner inputs, fewer triggers, calmer visuals, repeatable rhythms, predictable small wins. That's why your kids felt it. That's why the air changed when you walked into their rooms. That's why Ethan relaxed faster. That's why Owen joked cleaner. That's why Connor drifted into your orbit with ease. That's why Anna leaned back after nine years of silence.

You didn't force your way into being a better father. You engineered it from the iPhone wallpaper to the treadmill to the seat you took at the dinner table. And the magic of it all?

Not one of these systems required a therapist, a retreat, or a dramatic life overhaul. Just a man quietly rearranging the room so the very best version of himself had space to emerge.

FIELD NOTES

The Lobster Ritual Was Never About Lobster

This is about emotional clarity, psychological safety.

Simple rituals. Calm preparation before you engage.

Creating peace instead of chasing it, designing

a moment you can actually enjoy. This is the
masculine the world never taught you.

A man who creates steadiness before stepping
into intimacy.

Your kids feel it.

Women feel it.

Strangers feel it.

You feel it.

2.0 didn't invent this. It revealed it.

The IKEA Run with Ethan

There are rites of passage no one talks about. Not the big ones.
The quiet ones. Like furnishing a half-empty apartment after
your marriage cracks open.

In those early divorce days, I was pinging the ex, worrying
about schedules, fearing I'd lose the kids in the shuffle. I needed
to find a place, get it furnished, and figure it all out on the fly.
The kids were all unsure what to do, but when I asked if someone
would come over, Ethan reached out. Ethan, the steady one.

Not sure if he cleared it with his mom or not but I headed over
to the house. No real plan. No script. One thing I really needed
was furniture and when I asked Ethan for help, he enthusiasti-
cally said yes.

He walked the IKEA aisles with me, pencil and IKEA order
pad in hand. A bed, a couch, a kitchen table, some flatware, the
small plant he found at the end. Two men choosing the first pieces

of my new life. Only when I checked out did reality hit. I'd driven to IKEA in an Acura TL.

No problem. Plan B on the fly. Ethan didn't mind any of it. I said I'd grab a U-Haul van up the road. He stayed behind with the furniture, unbothered, steady, anchored. Three ninety-minute trips back and forth—van, apartment, return—and I had a place to sit, eat, sleep, and breathe. I might not remember what we ate. I might not remember the night around it. But I remember Ethan:

Calm. Steady.
Zero drama. Zero fear.

A quiet man code of his own: "We'll figure it out." And we did. Every time I look at the breakfast table or the old couch, I remember that my first apartment after the divorce didn't get built alone. It came together piece by piece, with a son beside me—steady, available—before I asked, before I knew how to ask, before I knew how much it mattered.

FIELD NOTES
Soft Eyes, Strong Spine Energy

Soft Eyes and Strong Spine = engineered calm = feminine trust

- You're not brittle
- You're not passive
- You're not controlling

- You are the intersection of masculinity and femininity

Women feel this instantly.

- Not always romantically—energetically
- People feel safe around men who pre-clear their internal chaos

The Czabe Ritual

There's another ritual that has been with me for almost twenty years, and it's one most people would never guess has anything to do with this book: a mildly popular radio show and podcast called *The Steve Czaban Show*.

Sports radio, technically. But really? A nervous-system refuge disguised as a guy talking about Aaron Rodgers, bad beats, and bits like "this might be a dumb question." Here's the thing: 2.0 men don't just meditate or journal. Sometimes their meditation is a voice on the radio or a podcast that feels familiar, steady, and predictable in all the right ways. That is what Czabe became.

After moving to North Carolina, my mornings were spent commuting down I-85, swallowed by traffic and static. I cycled through the usual radio suspects—*Mike & Mike*, Cowherd, fantasy football talk, even the occasional yacht rock when things felt absurd enough to warrant it. Then one morning, scanning through the noise, I landed on Fox Sports Radio—and there he was: *The Steve Czaban Show*.

I didn't know it yet, but this man was about to become one of the quiet architects of my emotional steadiness. He was witty. Sarcastic. Self-aware in a way most sports guys aren't. A little Boston-coded in spirit, even if he was D.C. by geography.

And he had bits, sound drops, quirky sayings, running jokes that made the whole show feel like a clubhouse: "Where you at? What you haulin'?," referring to himself as "Skeve Czaban..." (thanks to a banner that once misspelled his name), "Phil, check your yard!" or his Lazy River Fridays. It just felt right.

It wasn't because he talked sports. It was because he had rhythm. A predictable cadence. Warm irreverence. A way of making even nothing sound like something. What I didn't understand then but do now was this: Czabe was regulating. He was a 2.0 nervous-system anchor before it even had a name.

The Show That Got Fired, Then Fired Again, and Why It Mattered

Here's where the parallel hits. Steve Czaban kept getting cut loose when lineups changed. National. Then back to local D.C. Then Milwaukee. Each time he found a new chair, the music stopped again. So he built something that didn't depend on a program director: a podcast, earned by showing up and stacking episodes until it lasted.

He couldn't seem to catch a break and still somehow kept landing upright. I knew that pattern. Layoffs. Pivots. Being the wrong guy in the wrong place at the wrong time. Getting cut loose by timing out of my control. Rebuilding anyway. Making something out of nothing.

While I was driving to customer plants, sitting in traffic, or slogging up and down the eastern seaboard, I'd tune in and there he'd be—doing the same damn thing men like us do every day. Showing up anyway. No whining. No self-pity. Just that familiar cadence that tells the nervous system, "We're okay."

The ALE Coin–Always Leave Early

When he spun off the *Czabecast* podcast, the early folks were self-declared "one percenters." The diehards who would hang around for every episode. That's when the ALE coin appeared and was offered by Czabe to the first 100 loyal fans.

Always Leave Early. On one side: Green. A a car peeling away. Go. Get out. Beat the traffic. On the other: Red. Stay. There might be a comeback. I was lucky enough to snag one of the hundred or so coins he made.

Mainly it was a funny way to decide if you should stay at the game or leave. But it became more than merch. It became a quiet man code that matched my own. "Know when to stay present. Know when to slip out early and protect your peace." You can love the game without sitting in gridlock after the final whistle.

On rough days during Covid, and another layoff with long afternoons with too much future in my head, I'd thumb that coin and hear Czabe's voice in my ear, steady as ever, doing what he always did. Making the world feel just ordered enough that I could laugh and keep going.

Why This Belongs in the
Life-in-Practice Section for Dads

This isn't nostalgia. This is neurology. Men desperately need anchors, rituals that do the emotional equivalent of lowering the heart rate. For some, it's lifting. For some, fishing. For some, meditation apps they pretend they use.

For me? Sometimes it was Czabe. A familiar voice in the chaos. A guy who took his lumps without making them everyone else's problem. A reminder that men survive by rhythm, not reinvention. This is the part dads don't get told: If you want to live at a healthy emotional frequency, you have to curate what comes into your brain.

And that includes a podcast that steadies you, voices that ground you, humor that resets the nervous system, predictable rhythms that become emotional ballast. It was never about sports talk. It was about this: Czabe kept me from drifting back into 1.0. And 2.0 knows a good anchor when it finds one.

The lobster ritual, every piece prepared before the first bite. Order before emotion, the nervous-system blueprint behind Soft Eyes, Strong Spine.

NOTES FROM A DIVORCED DAD
What to Carry Forward

- Ritual is how values travel without lectures
- Repetition creates safety and meaning
- Small moments build a man's culture at home
- The point isn't the lobster, it's the signal
- Your kids remember who you were when
  you did it

THE LINES YOUR KIDS NEVER FORGET

Words That Become a Way of Life

Every dad thinks his kids are going to remember the big speeches. The "sit down, this is serious" talks. The car rides where you tried to open their eyes to life. The moment on the back deck where you poured out your heart like a Hallmark movie and waited for music to swell behind you.

They might remember some of that. But what really sticks is the stuff that sneaks into their twenties and thirties and follows them into jobs, marriages, airports, and the quiet moments when they're alone—and it almost never comes from the big moments.

It comes from the throwaway lines. The nicknames. The emojis. The weird little family phrases. The songs that played in the background while everyone was half-awake with toast crumbs on the counter.

Legacy doesn't sound like a rehearsed speech; it sounds like the one-liner you've said a hundred times and barely remember. Your kids remember it for you.

This chapter is about that language—the lines, sounds, and small family codes that become portable inheritance. The real stuff. The lived stuff. The "we say that in our family" stuff. And here's the cool insight underneath all of it: Your kids don't inherit your advice. They inherit your defaults.

Your default tone. Your default reaction. Your default way of handling tension. Your default way of returning to calm. Those defaults don't show up as speeches. They show up as phrases, little repeated moves that carry your whole operating system in five words or less.

A Dadism is not a slogan. It is a frequency container. It holds calm or tightening, hospitality or control, humor or avoidance, confidence or performance. Your kids may forget the whole conversation, but they'll remember the container. That's why the lines matter.

The Handle Theory

I didn't grow up thinking about "legacy." I grew up thinking about getting through the week, keeping the peace, and being the kind of guy who doesn't make life harder for anybody. I did grow up around a man who understood something about language. My dad had a way of taking a normal moment and giving it a handle. A handle is what lets you carry a heavy thing without cutting your hands.

Tom gave people handles all day long. If he leaned in with that half-grin and said your name drawn out, with that deep, raspy delivery, you knew something was coming. Not a lecture. More like a little piece of reality wrapped in humor with a soft landing built in. Sometimes it was just noise. A one-liner. A throwaway.

Sometimes it was the whole mood of the room shifting because he made it safe to laugh. And sometimes it was love disguised as a joke, because that's what his generation did. Tom could say the same word three different ways and mean three different things.

"Ricky." (pay attention)

"Riiicky." (I'm about to tell you something you'll like)

"RICKY." (write this down, this matters)

Same word. Different frequency. That's the first lesson of dad language. Kids don't hear words first. They feel tone first. And if you want to know what your kids will remember, don't just listen to what you say. Listen to how you say it.

Where Dad Lines Are Born

Most of the lines your kids carry forward are born in three places. Either the car, the kitchen, or in chaos. No eye-contact pressure. No "look at me while I talk to you" energy. Just a windshield, a road, and the weird honesty that shows up when a nervous system feels safe.

Kitchens—because you're half-awake, the cereal is out, someone's late, someone's hungry, and someone's annoyed. You're trying to keep it moving without making it a thing. As someone tries to cut a corner to save time, you throw out:

"Do it right or do it twice."

You're not being dramatic. Emotion is a highlighter. The moment has heat, and whatever you say in that heat often gets recorded as law.

That's why Dadisms matter. They're what your kids reach for later when the moment has heat and you're not there.

Car Rides: The Chapel of Dadisms

When the kids were younger, we lived in the car—swim practice, basketball, baseball, school. With four kids spread across six years, there was a stretch when something was happening every day. We'd split up, but I usually had at least a couple of kids with me as we ran the loop from one game to the next.

It felt hectic, but the world was simple in a way I didn't fully appreciate until later. Before Owen started high school, I helped coach his baseball teams. We didn't win much, but the kids kept showing up and playing hard. We'd face travel teams who treated the Gastonia Rec League like a training ground. It made that league sharp, and our small-town team rarely stood much of a chance.

We had a blast though, and I still have a picture of Owen I cherish from the year he decided to give catching a try. Big smile behind a filthy uniform after the game. I was still in 1.0 in those days, so not the best coach looking back. A bit tense but we still had a blast.

We would often stop at Sonic and get grape slushies for the drive back home. Often Connor was in tow as well, while Ethan and Anna were at swim practice at a pool nearby.

We would talk some about the games, but often it would drift to dad-type conversations, and I'd hear myself say things I didn't even mean to, like "that's why they call it an accident and not an on purpose," or "they say a broken clock is right twice a day," or maybe just something totally off-the-wall goofy.

You never knew what I would come up with. At some point we got to talking about Norm Macdonald's bit on SNL doing Burt Reynolds and "Turd Ferguson." That led to something we still do today. Anytime there is anyone or anything with a name that resembles Ferguson in any way, it is always followed up with "Turd Ferguson, it's a funny name."

When they start to quote your Dadisms back, you realize they were listening. And soaking it in. Not a sermon. Not some big fatherly moment. Just a line that came out because you've got a kid who's trying to do things fast, and you're trying to teach him that fast is fine until fast makes you sloppy and you have to do it again anyway.

That line has survived. Not because it's clever. Because it's short and clean and it lands in real life. I can see Owen, now grown, moving through the world with that steady competence, and I can hear that line inside him. Not in a robotic way. In a values way. That's what dads underestimate.

A Specific Car Ride (So the Idea Has Bones)

It's a warm, sticky spring afternoon in Gastonia. The sun is already doing its work—I feel it the second I step outside. We're in the car heading to baseball practice. Owen's in the passenger seat, glove on his lap, chewing a wad of Big League Chew like it's a job.

Looking back as we drive, I notice something small but unfamiliar. I'm less hyper-vigilant. Less busy in my head. I'm not working two steps ahead of a problem I imagine might be coming next.

I didn't know it at the time, but that's what it felt like to be becoming the person I was meant to be. The foggy old lens giving way to something cleaner. Clearer. A way of being that left more room for connection.

I've got one hand on the wheel. The radio is low. Not because we're having a deep talk; it just happens to be that way. We pull up to a stoplight, and I glance over and see him doing that kid thing where he's trying to look relaxed while his nervous system is running.

He's not saying it. But his body is. I could have done what 1.0 dads do and tried to fix the feeling. "You nervous?" "You're going to do great." "Remember what I told you last time." "Here's a whole paragraph on confidence."

But this time, I just kept it normal. Glancing over at his hat, I bring up Turd Ferguson with something deliberate like "Man, that's a big hat." He smirks. Not because it's hilarious. Because it's familiar. Because it's our code. He gives a quick, "Ha, it's a funny name." Then I add one more sentence, soft, almost throwaway:

"Just have fun."

And then I shut up. That's the whole move. A clean line. A small confidence signal. Space. At the field, he goes and does his thing. This was toward the end of our baseball years, and it was how I would align the emotional pace of the last months of a five-year run of games. It should have been sooner, but better to learn along the way and create more space.

Some days he had some hits. Some days he didn't. Some days

he was a little in his head and I could see it. But the point was never the outcome. The point was that, in his nervous system, he started to see a father who didn't make the moment heavier.

He now had a father who offered a handle, then let him carry it. That's what kids remember. We think values are taught with big talks. But values get built the way houses get built—one board at a time, one repeated phrase at a time, in ordinary moments.

The Near-Miss Line

Some lines are born in adrenaline. We had one that became a family reset phrase, part joke, part gratitude, part "holy hell, that could have been bad."

"We almost got crushed."

It came out after the near-miss in traffic I mentioned earlier. The kind where your heart spikes, your hands clamp the wheel, and nobody speaks for three seconds because you're still doing the math of what almost happened.

Then the exhale hits, and the nervous system wants to dump the energy. And instead of turning it into drama, we turned it into a line. That line did something important. It acknowledged the danger. It released it. It let us move forward without tensing for the next twenty minutes.

That's a Tom move, by the way. Laugh after chaos. Not because you're minimizing it, because you're refusing to live in the grip. A lot of dads think being "serious" is how you keep kids safe. Sometimes it is, but only in a precise instant.

But there's also a kind of safety your kids need that is quieter. They need you to show them how to return to calm. A line like "we almost got crushed" isn't just humor. It's a demonstration. Yes, life is real. Yes, things can happen. And yes, we come back down.

FIELD NOTES
How a Dad Line Becomes a Forever Line

A dad line becomes a forever line when it has three things:

- It's short—If it needs a paragraph, it won't survive.
- It's clean—No shame. No sting. No manipulation.
- It lands in a moment of emotion—Fear. Pride. Relief. Disappointment. Joy.

That's when the nervous system records it.
That's why lectures fail. They're too long and too tightened.

Dadisms succeed because they're small and relaxed:

- They slip past the defenses
- They become part of the kid

"Honest People are Allowed
to Have Short Memories"

This one started as a joke. One of those moments where a kid borderline told the truth, but you can feel the loophole energy in the room. Instead of turning it into a courtroom scene, you drop the line, "Honest people are allowed to have short memories."

Everyone laughs. But then it sticks. I wasn't even sure if I had heard it or made it up on the spot, but it has lasted because underneath the laugh is something real: If you're honest, you don't have to track lies. If you're straight, you don't have to manage versions of yourself. If you tell the truth, your nervous system can stay calmer.

That's not morality talk.
That's practical peace.

And the deeper part, the part I didn't recognize until I started living in 2.0, is that this line is also a message to your kids. "I'd rather you tell the truth and move forward than hide and carry it alone."

That matters. Because kids aren't just learning rules. They're learning what kind of home truth lives in.

Does truth get punished? Does truth get mocked? Does truth get used against you? Or does truth get met with steadiness and a reset? A one-liner can build that culture.

"Unintended Consequences"

This is one of those ultimate dad phrases you say when someone tries to fix something but in the end makes it worse. Not an original, but one that gets used often. It's also the phrase you say to yourself when your 1.0 wiring tries to sprint ahead of your best judgment.

It's playful. It's a warning. It's also self-awareness in five syllables. Unintended consequences. That's what happens when you over-text. Over-explain. Over-react. Over-parent.

You intend to connect.
You intend to help.
You intend to be present.

And you accidentally drain the moment. You make it heavy. You make your kid feel managed. So sometimes the line isn't just for your kids. It's for you.

It's a reminder to slow down and ask, "What happens if I don't fix this? What happens if I just stay calm and let the moment breathe?" That's 2.0 fatherhood.

"Measure Twice, Cut Once"

The old carpenter line from middle-school shop class turns into a nervous-system rule. A lot of fatherhood—especially divorced fatherhood—happens in texts. Texts are where 1.0 dads blow it.

They type fast. They type long. They type emotional.
They type like they're trying to win the moment.

"Measure twice, cut once" is a ritual line. It means, Pause. Read it again. Ask what you're trying to accomplish. Make sure the tone is clean.

If you've ever sent a text that felt good in your fingers and terrible the next morning, you know what I mean. Measure twice. Cut once.

FIELD NOTES
The Texting Ritual
(Where Dads Win or Lose the Whole Day)

If you're a divorced dad, or any type of parent, you know this truth. A text can change the weather.

- One sentence can turn a day into connection
- One sentence can turn a day into friction
- One extra paragraph can turn "close" into "please stop"

That's why "measure twice, cut once" isn't just a clever line used many times with your kids. In the posture of Soft Eyes, Strong Spine, it can became a ritual. Here's what it looks like in real life:

You're about to send a text
You feel a little heat
You feel that 1.0 urge to explain yourself
into safety

So you pause. You read it again. You ask "Is this about my anxiety or their life?"

Then you cut it down to the clean version.

The clean version is one sentence. Warmth. No hook. No pressure.

- "Proud of you"
- "Thinking of you. No need to respond."
- "Hope today goes easy"

That's the kind of text that builds closeness because it says "I'm here."

And it also says "I'm not trying to pull you toward me." That's Strong Spine.

And if you do this long enough, your kids learn something without you ever teaching it directly.

- Connection doesn't require pressure
- Love doesn't require performance
- Closeness can be light. That's a forever lesson.

"Type That into Your Google Machine"

This one is pure dad energy. I picked this one up along the way. They always knew what it meant and it stuck. But it also carries something healthy.

"I trust you to figure it out."

"I'm not the oracle."

"You don't need me to be."

There's a quiet maturity in a dad who doesn't need to be the answer to everything. Kids don't need a father who knows everything.

They need a father who's steady enough to let them learn.

The Emoji Dialect

Every family invents a language. Ours has evolved to memes since we all have cell phones. We have the usual "Peter Griffin's bent-backwards knee" if anyone gets hurt. But the language also has emojis.

Somewhere along the way, someone used the cowboy hat emoji, mostly due to its low hit rate. Who uses the cowboy hat emoji and why would you? Who even knows what it symbolizes other than a really happy cowboy. A moment later, someone replied with an even more obscure emoji.

🤠 and 🤨 became shorthand for a whole emotional paragraph.

🤠 isn't just "cowboy."
It's "I'm good."
It's "I love you."
It's "no drama."
It's "I'm proud."
It's "I'm here."
It's "I don't need anything from you."

😳 is the sarcastic cousin.

The "you're killing me" energy.

The "this is ridiculous" wink.

The little face you send when you're calling balls and strikes without making it a fight.

That's the beauty of small language. It lets you be present without being heavy. There are moments when a kid doesn't want a speech. He wants a signal.

A clean check-in. A little warmth that doesn't turn into an emotional negotiation. That's what the emoji does.

Heng Dai: A Whole Sentence in Two Words

We say "Heng dai" in our family. It's a random Chinese saying we "borrowed" from *Deadwood*. If you're not us, it probably sounds like nothing.

In the show, it had to do with loyalty and brotherhood. We found a photo of the character with his fingers crossed, and it felt right. The phrase fell out of someone's mouth one day and never left.

But that's exactly how family language forms. A phrase shows up. It carries a feeling. It gets repeated. It becomes shorthand for a whole emotional paragraph.

For us, "Heng dai" is a kind of brotherhood signal. It's the nod. It's the "I'm with you." It's the "no big speech needed." It's the "I love you, but I'm going to keep my dignity and not turn this into a Hallmark commercial."

So when I send a cowboy hat emoji or drop a "Heng dai," I'm doing the same move in modern form. And here's what I want dads to hear: You don't have to become a poet. You don't have to become a therapist. You don't have to become a different personality. You just have to build a few clean signals your kids can trust.

Signals that mean "I'm here. I'm calm. I'm proud. I'm not trying to control you. I don't need you to manage my emotions." That's what kids feel as safety. And safety is what turns a dad-relationship into something durable.

Because kids grow up. They move away. They get their own lives. The relationship survives on small signals more than big conversations. A quick line. A shared phrase. A two-word code that says "we're still us."

The odd phrases and emojis let us do that. If you tried to explain this to an outsider, it would sound ridiculous. But your kids know exactly what it means.

Sunday Language: Fantasy Football and the Running Commentary

If you want to understand how men pass down language, watch them watch sports. Not the screaming-at-the-TV guys. I mean the quieter version, the running commentary, the one-liners, the little bursts of humor that make a three-hour game feel like a shared experience instead of just noise. The group chat thread.

When the boys and I watch the Bruins, the Red Sox, or any Boston team, there is always that underlayer of talk. Not therapy talk. Not feelings talk. Just that easy "we're here together" talk.

A quick call on a penalty. A sarcastic line about a coach's decision. A little "LFG" when you feel the momentum shift. And then, because the Brockman family can't help itself, there are the phrases that became permanent. Some are local to Boston sports, but it's things like "Sox kids eat free" if the Sox won or the Peter Griffin soccer horn GIF when Pavel Zacha scores. A big "Pritch Please" at just the right moment.

It sounds dumb written out. But that's the point. Men love through the dumb stuff. They do closeness through shared humor. They do safety through predictability. They do connection through repetition. That's why Dadisms matter. They're not just words.

They're a recurring bridge. And this is where Tom shows up again, quietly, under the surface. Tom filled rooms with those little bridges. He didn't ask you to "talk about your feelings." He made it easy to breathe around him.

He carried the awkward gap. He gave the moment a handle. He kept the room warm without turning it into a production. So when the kids and I sit there on a Sunday and text clips and one-liners, that's not just sports.

That's lineage.

The Gifts That Become Mementos

Sometimes your kids don't quote you. They hand you something. A photo. A framed memory. A little object that sits on your desk and quietly says, "We know you." One year, the boys got me a Boston Garden photo from game six of the 2011 Cup run.

That wasn't just a hockey thing. It was a declaration. "We see what you love. We know what lights you up. We're paying attention."

Sometimes they talk you into buying gifts for yourself. Like the turntable we got. Old school, new age. Connor talked me into it. We stream YouTube Music most of the time, but that turntable is a ritual object. You drop the needle and it slows the whole house down by two clicks. It makes music intentional again. It turns "background noise" into "we're here."

That's fatherhood in a sentence. You buy something for the house, and these unique artifacts matter because they create another kind of dad language.

The house takes on a calm, safe, comfortable vibe. Not from what you say. From how your home feels.

Because your kids don't just remember your lines. They remember your atmosphere. That's the point.

Music: The Other Language

If you saw me from across a terminal—North Face zipped, beard a little grey, head nodding to a beat you can't hear—you might think I'm somewhere else.

But I'm not. I'm exactly where the music is. Music gives me two lives at once—the outer one people see and the inner one that's always been mine. It didn't start with vinyl, or with a turntable in a quiet Gastonia house. It started on Long Pine Road in Sharon, Massachusetts, when a tired little boy—too alone for how young he was—dragged a Boston Globe bag along a dark New England street.

Snow crunching under Marshalls boots. Streetlights humming. An original Walkman with both AM/FM radio and a cassette tucked inside my winter jacket. I didn't know it then, but I was already building it. A life I could live inside of, one song at a time.

Music as Structure,
Survival, and a Soft Place to Stand

People think music is entertainment. For me, it was architecture. When the childhood house felt loud, unpredictable, or emotionally cluttered, music became the room I could go into where no one else had the key.

Every kid from a house like that learns to find structure somewhere. Some choose sports. Some choose grades. Some choose rebellion. I chose rhythm.

- Long Pine Road – Boston, Lou Reed, anything with a beat
- College dorm hallways – U2, The Cure, Guns N' Roses bleeding under the doors
- Rocking babies – "Somewhere Over the Rainbow" loop, the many versions
- Cross-country flights – Stones, Black Crowes, anything that quickened the miles
- The divorce years – Some Willie Nelson or whatever could make minutes hurt less

Music wasn't escape. It was scaffolding. The first thing that ever told me, "You can feel something without being crushed by it."

The Morning Playlist That
Accidentally Became Family Culture

If my kids remember anything about my houses in those early years after the divorce, I hope it's this: The mornings with the playlist. It didn't start as a ritual. It started because we were tired.

It was a townhouse off Rocky Falls in 2018. Two or three school mornings a week when the kids were with me. The house wasn't loud, but the energy could shift fast—teeth not brushed, homework not finished, someone missing a shoe. One morning, before the scramble could take over, I opened YouTube Music and typed "morning songs" and a playlist popped up, "Songs to Raise Your Kids To."

I didn't create the playlist. I didn't overthink it. I just tapped the first one that looked halfway promising. It was perfect. A playlist with just the right kind of warmth. "Boogie Wonderland," "You Can Call Me Al," "Dream On," "Take Me Home, Country Roads," "Shining Star," "We Didn't Start the Fire." Classics. High-spirited. Steady rhythm. Zero chaos.

Not indie whisper tracks. Not brooding acoustic. Not "curated vibes." Just warmth, wrapped in familiar melodies. I'd light a scented candle, hit shuffle, and the house would shift from morning scramble to something like … ease.

The "Yeah, No" Moment

When Connor started his junior year in fall 2024 and I moved into a nicer, bigger place, I thought, *Maybe I'll switch it up. Fresh year. New playlist.* I found another YouTube Music list with more modern tracks he liked. Same general vibe. Same pace, just refreshed.

In my head, it was an upgrade. Look at Dad, staying current. The second Connor walked down the stairs and heard it playing,

I wasn't so sure. He went about his morning and finished up getting ready and started to head out the door.

On the way out, I stopped Connor and asked, "Hey, what do you think of the new playlist?" He didn't answer. He just paused heading out the door, then turned and gave the slow teenage head shake that you have seen before and translates to "yeah, no." Message received.

Next morning, I went right back to the OG playlist. Candle lit. Coffee brewing. And the whole house slid back into the rhythm that feels like home. Because it turns out, the playlist was never about the songs. It was about the ritual that held us steady.

If Dadisms are the lines your kids quote, music is the atmosphere they grow up inside. I didn't realize how much it had become part of our family's glue until I heard it echoed back at me—the morning playlist playing while the kids got ready for school.

And it's deep as hell. Because music doesn't just fill a room. It sets a frequency. A calmer frequency. A "life is still good" frequency.

Concerts: When Your Kid Becomes Your Buddy for Three Hours

Concerts are a strange fatherhood laboratory. You're standing next to your kid in a crowd. No chores. No school forms. No logistics to manage. Just two people inside the same song, reacting in real time, shoulder to shoulder.

The kids started finding their way into that world on their own. Ethan wound up at Lollapalooza. Owen and Connor went to their first show together—Black Pistol Fire. Loud, cramped, unforgettable. They all love live music. I've never had to push that. I just make room for it whenever I can.

Connor is wired differently. Music doesn't just land on him—it pulls him in. He picked up a sax and joined the marching band. Talked me into a turntable. He's the one who follows bands the long way, tracking releases and tours, waiting for the next time the Black Keys come through.

They were supposed to play Charlotte one year, but the show got canceled. It was rescheduled in Myrtle Beach the summer before Connor's senior year. Life intervened. His friend got grounded. His brother ended up in Europe. Connor looked at me and said, "You want to go?"

And I was thinking: *Yes. Obviously yes.* Even though I hadn't been to a concert in years. I used to go all the time back in the day. But somewhere along the way adulthood turned into "maybe next time" and then I looked up and it had been a decade since I'd taken the young kids to see Bruce Springsteen and screamed Badlands off key in their ears.

So we go. We're walking in with the crowd, and it's that familiar electricity—lights, voices, people buzzing like they're about to be part of something. And the whole time I'm watching Connor.

Not in a creepy "dad surveillance" way. More like … gratitude. Because this is the goal. This is the thing. Not that your kid obeys you. Not that your kid needs you. That your kid chooses you. Even if you were third choice, he still chose you. He wants you next to him in a room full of noise.

The Black Keys come out and they're incredible. We are fifteen rows back from the stage. Connor is fired up. I'm lit up. And for three hours that night the world is simple. We are just two guys having a good time.

No over-parenting. No fixing. Just presence. That is fatherhood as a ritual. Not a big emotional conversation. A shared moment that says "we're good."

And in the morning, when you're replaying it in your head, you realize. Music is one of the quiet ways kids keep a relationship alive. It gives you a lane where you don't have to be profound. You just have to be there. That's why those kitchen playlists matter. They're not background. They're relationship glue.

The Brockman Language

Brockman dads have their own language:

Tone over content.
Humor as hospitality.
Small habits become family memory.

We use humor to make people comfortable. Not to be the center of attention, but as a way of saying, "You're safe here. We can breathe. We can laugh. We can keep going."

That energy made its way into my house. And it shows up in weird little ways. Sometimes it's a one-liner. Sometimes it's a goofy meme. Sometimes it's an eye roll that says "we're not doing a whole production about this."

Those tiny moves are what kids remember. Not because they're profound. Because they're consistent.

Aisles and Attention

In hindsight, there were places I witnessed emotional availability long before I had language for it. One of them showed up during a weekly errand run as a kid.

Back in the late '70s, my dad started doing the food shopping. What began as a one-off turned into a weekly rhythm. I went with him every time. It became its own Saturday ritual: a man who grew up in the '50s heading to Stop & Shop to do the week's shopping.

That might sound small, but for a kid, those trips are where you learn how a man moves through the world—what he notices, how he treats people, what his nervous system does in public. Tom in a grocery store was … Tom. He was always carrying the conversation. Always making people feel comfortable. The other ladies couldn't believe this guy was doing the grocery shopping. They'd chat him up. He'd chat them up right back, not flirt-flirt, more like warm-human.

And standing there next to him, I learned something I didn't have language for at the time. A man can be masculine and still be socially soft.

He can be steady and still be easy.

He can be competent and still be playful.

He can make people feel safe without being a performer.

That's what I mean when I say Part IV is ritual. It's not "be a better man." It's "build the kind of daily tone that makes your kids want to be near you."

Because kids learn that tone first in ordinary places. Parking lots. Grocery aisles. Checkout lines. The way you talk to strangers. The way you treat the tired cashier. The way you hold your own mood.

And then without you realizing it, your kids bring that tone into their own adult life. That's the transmission. Not a speech. A vibe. A frequency.

FIELD NOTES
The Language of Dads

Dad language tends to fall into three categories.

Reset Lines—These are the ones that pull the nervous system back down:

- "We almost got crushed"
- "Alright, we're good"
- "Breathe"
- A simple cowboy hat emoji

Reset lines keep a moment from becoming a spiral.

Courage Lines—These are the ones that help a kid move toward something hard:

- "Honest people are allowed to have short memories"
- "Ten pounds of potatoes in a five-pound bag"
- "Not my monkey, not my circus"

Courage lines aren't hype. They're permission.

Belonging Lines—These are the ones that say, "You're one of us":

- Nicknames
- Inside jokes
- Memes and viral clips
- The songs you play in the kitchen
- The way you say their name

Belonging lines are not advice. They're home.

If you're a dad reading this, here's a simple practice.

Don't try to manufacture lines; that gets corny fast.
Instead, notice what category the moment needs
Does this moment need a reset? Does it need courage? Does it need belonging?
Then speak one clean sentence and let the rest be silence.

That's how you stay 2.0. Soft Eyes, Strong Spine.
Short line. Space after.

The Space After the Line

This is the part most dads miss. A Dadism isn't just what you say. It's what you don't do after you say it. If you drop a clean line and then hover, you just turned it into control. If you drop a clean line and then keep talking, you just turned it into a lecture.

If you drop a clean line and then demand a reaction, you just turned it into performance.

The power of a Dadism is the space after it. Drop a line, let it land, let the room laugh, and then move on. Don't squeeze the moment. That's Strong Spine. Not rigidity, restraint. If you want the line to become inheritance, here's the secret:

Say it.
Then release it.

Let your kid own it.
Let your kid pick it up later.
Let your kid carry it in his own way.

That's how you avoid turning "dad language" into "dad pressure."

The Moment I Read Owen's Text

Earlier I mentioned the heartfelt text Owen sent. Flip back if you need to find it. It really struck a chord. I remember exactly where I was when I read it. A normal day where your mind is on a hundred things. My phone buzzes. I glance down. And I see Owen's name. I expect a clip. A joke. A quick question. Instead, I see a paragraph.

And there's that first line, something like, "I know we don't talk too serious ..." That's how you know it's real. When a kid announces that he's stepping out of his usual lane, it means he's about to risk something. I read it once fast. Then I read it again slower.

And by the time I hit the part about car rides and values and "I quote you," my throat does that thing where it tightens like it's trying to hold emotion back out of habit. Because dads don't get a lot of report cards like that.

You get grades in silence. You get grades in whether they show up. Whether they call. Whether they still want to be near you. Whether they look relaxed around you. But you don't often get the words. And when you do, it hits like a weight coming off your chest that you didn't even realize you were carrying.

I didn't jump into a long reply. That's the old me. The over-explainer. The guy who turns a clean moment into a whole emotional thread. I just wrote back something simple. Proud. Grateful. Love you. And then I let it breathe.

Because the whole point of this chapter is the thing I had to learn the hard way. When your kid offers you something clean, don't smother it with your relief.

That landed like proof. Not proof that I was perfect. Proof that the small things counted. Proof that the lines went in. And it made me realize something else: Sometimes we spend years judging our fatherhood by the wrong scoreboard.

We judge it by the fights we had. The days we blew it. The stretches we were stressed and distracted and not our best. But your kids, if you're doing it right, are often judging you by something quieter: Did you give them language they could stand on?

RITUAL RUNWAY:
How to Build This Without Trying Too Hard

If you're reading this and thinking, "Okay, but I

don't have any Dadisms," you do. You just don't notice them yet. Here's a simple runway to bring this into your own house without forcing it:

Listen for what you repeat—For a week, notice what comes out of your mouth on autopilot. You will be surprised how consistent you are when someone spills something. When someone is late. When someone is anxious. When someone is proud. When someone is sad. Write down the phrases. Don't judge them yet. Just notice them.

Ask yourself, "Does this line create calm or pressure?"—Some lines are neutral. Some lines are helpful. Some lines are little grenades. You can tell by the kid's body. Do they soften? Or do they tense? A good Dadism makes a kid's shoulders drop by one inch.

Keep the ones you would want quoted back to you—This is the best filter in the world. Would you be proud to hear this line coming out of your kid's mouth at twenty-eight? If yes, keep it. If no, let it go.

Upgrade the bad lines to clean lines—A lot of dads have a default line like, "What the hell are you doing?" Upgrade it to something that keeps the

connection intact. "Slow down." "Try again."
"Let's fix it." Same message. Different frequency.

Leave space after you speak—This is the last step, and it's the one that separates 1.0 fatherhood from 2.0. Say the line. Then stop. Let the kid breathe. Let the moment unfold. Let them carry it. That's how the line becomes inheritance instead of pressure.

That's the runway. And here's the secret bonus. When you start doing this, you'll realize you're not just giving your kids language. You're giving yourself a calmer life.

The Other Side: When a Line Becomes Too Much

Now, because this book isn't a cheerleading session, I have to talk about the other side. A line can soothe, but it can also smother. A joke can bond, but it can also invade. A saying can guide, but it can also control. If you've ever been a 1.0 dad, you know exactly what I mean.

1.0 dads use language to manage the moment. To smooth it. To make the discomfort go away. To fix the feeling before the kid even knows what he's feeling.

2.0 dads use language differently. They use it as a signal. A steadying hand on the shoulder. Then they give the kid space.

The difference between legacy and over-parenting isn't the

language you use, it's the space you give. Which means the next step in fatherhood isn't learning what to say. It's learning how to stand back far enough for your kids to come forward.

You've built the language. You've built the atmosphere. Now you learn the quieter art: how to raise good kids without over-parenting them.

NOTES FROM A DIVORCED DAD
What to Carry Forward

- Kids remember tone longer than they remember wording
- A line spoken from calm lands deeper than a paragraph from tension
- "Small" words can carry a lifetime of meaning
- Your best lines aren't clever, they're true
- What you say once can echo for years

RAISE THEM, DON'T CHASE THEM

Prescence Beats Perfection

Dads rarely admit to being needy. The word feels too exposed, like something that doesn't belong in everyday conversation. But real dad-neediness isn't dramatic. It's subtle. It's energetic.

It's the emotional lean-in behind every text. It's the invisible pull in your voice when you ask about their day. It's the unspoken hope behind every moment. "Please give me something that makes me feel okay." It's unintentional. It's understandable. And it's the number one reason good fathers accidentally create distance with their kids.

The cure isn't coldness. The cure isn't withdrawal. The cure is clarity. Calm. A grounded nervous system. The shift into 2.0. When you stop asking your kids to regulate your emotional state, they finally trust you with theirs.

I'll say this as clean as I can: A lot of over-parenting is just a dad trying to get a receipt for love. A second text that doesn't need to exist. A follow-up question that is really a fishing line. A "just checking in" that is really "please don't forget me." I know that move because I lived that move.

When I started shifting into 2.0, I began practicing a tiny discipline that felt almost stupid at first and then felt like freedom. The Let-It-Sit Rule: If I send the text, I let it sit. No second ping. No question mark. No extra paragraph to soften it. I let my kid's nervous system breathe without me climbing into it.

The first few times I did that, my body felt like it was missing something, like I'd forgotten my wallet. That's the addiction of over-functioning. You don't realize you're hooked until you try to stop.

And then something happened. The replies that came back felt clean. Not because they were longer. Because they were unpressured.

The Two-Text Rule

If you send one text, let the next move be theirs. Not as a game. As a gift of space. If they don't reply, you didn't fail. You simply didn't invade.

Presence is not volume. A father's presence has nothing to do with noise or effort. It isn't measured in how many texts he sends. It isn't how many questions he fires off after school. It isn't how many plans he proposes or how intensely he tries to stay involved.

Presence is measured by one thing. "Can my kid breathe in the room with me?" If the answer is yes, you're doing it right.

If the answer is no, no amount of "but I love you!" will fix the frequency mismatch. Kids don't move toward the parent who fills the air. They move toward the one who calms it.

A recent hockey game was a solid lesson in 2.0 presence. It happened during a Bruins game, in one of those tiny father-son micro-moments that would've gone unnoticed back in 1.0. Owen texted me a quick update. Just a ping. A thread of connection tossed into the night. Old me would've grabbed it with both hands. "Yeah! Great play! How's school? Did you eat? Any tests coming up?"

I would've turned a spark into a spotlight out of love, but also out of fear. 2.0 did something different. I matched his energy: light, warm, easy. A single calm reply. No elongation. No invisible pressure. No grabbing the moment and making it bigger than it was. And that one clean reply did more bonding than ten emotional paragraphs ever could.

Kids lean toward gravity not turbulence. That's fatherhood's unspoken physics. People don't remember the paragraph. They remember the feeling. These are lived truths that rewired my entire fatherhood:

Don't elongate a moment.
Small moments stay small; that's what makes them safe.

Give without drawing tight.
If you can't give something without attaching expectation, don't give it yet.

Show up without forcing resonance.
Your kid's vibe is not a performance review of your parenting.

Let the text sit.

Silence isn't rejection. It's space.

Let the child lead.

Their momentum is ten times stronger than anything you manufacture.

Trust the quiet.

Kids don't quote speeches. They quote stability.

Know When Less is More

Texting is mentioned often in these chapters as it is such a large part of how we all interact. It is work and personal life beyond our kids. Relationships and dating have endless text traps someone prone to overcorrecting can fall into.

My texts don't save the planet. Often they are just simple messages about sports or gambling. One particular night I got a text from my friend Matt, who'd hit a wild parlay. It was one of those bets that makes no sense until the payout screen lights up. He texted the win, proud and riding high.

I was super psyched for him and totally pumped he'd shared the win with me. This is where you can completely block the connection by being way off on emotional frequency. That includes all the unintended consequences I mentioned along the way. There was a sense of wanting to join the excitement, as one of the boys had coincidently hit a decent size parlay that weekend.

This would have been a harmless share. I wasn't trying to brag. But it would have shifted the tone and missed the original intent of his text.

That might sound like too much thought put into a simple exchange. But it's a clean example of how easy it is to miss frequency.

Old me would've jumped in with my kid's win too. Not out of ego. Out of wanting to share a moment. Out of wanting to stay connected. Out of that old reflex to match energy with energy.

But 2.0 stayed still. Let Matt have his moment. No topping. No spotlight shift. No "look at us!" reflex. And the restraint landed deeper than I expected.

Because a man who doesn't steal momentum from adults doesn't steal it from his kids either. That's what non-invasive fatherhood looks like in the wild.

FIELD NOTES
What Over-Parenting Really Is

Over-parenting isn't involvement. It isn't effort.
It isn't even presence.
Over-parenting is trying to manage your child's
feelings so you don't have to feel your own.

When you stop doing that, when you let your kid
have their emotions without fixing, steering, or
interpreting, they develop something priceless—
self-trust.

Kids don't say "thank you for the emotional
stability, Dad." They say it differently:

- They wander into your room and flop onto the couch
- They send random photos from college
- They call you about nothing
- They invite you in without fear of being smothered

That's the Quiet Backbone, the emotional architecture they grow around without ever using that language.
A father with a Quiet Backbone isn't controlling—not reactive. Not performative. Not needy.
He's steady. And kids build their entire adult nervous systems around that steadiness.

Ethan and the Valedictorian Lesson

Ethan has always moved with a quiet steadiness. He learned how to stay with things. Followed through. Spent long stretches absorbed in what he was building and learning. That consistency showed up again and again.

When he graduated valedictorian of his high school, it felt fully earned. The groundwork had been there for years. Dual enrollment at the local college. Honors classes stacked like scaffolding. A GPA well north of 4.0. He did the work. And the work mattered.

And yet at the time I didn't celebrate it loudly enough in my heart. I appreciated the achievement. I bragged to anyone that would listen and framed the program from the day. But I never celebrated his victory internally as I could have.

Years later I realized the deeper truth. Ethan didn't rise in spite of me. He didn't rise because of me. He rose alongside me. He was mirroring the man I was trying to become long before I even knew 2.0 existed.

He taught me something without ever saying a word. Kids thrive in the spaces you don't rush to fill. Ethan has always been the quiet kind of steady. Not the kid who needs a big reaction. Not the kid who wants you narrating his identity in real time.

If you push too hard with a kid like Ethan, he doesn't fight you, he just disappears a little. That's his boundary. It's clean. It's respectful. It's also a master class if you're paying attention. The best thing I ever learned with him was simple—show up … and then get out of the way.

The Breaststroke Gold, an Ethan Classic

Since we've touched on Ethan, I have to provide one of Ethan's all time "yeah, I got this" moments. It was back when he was about thirteen. In those days, he and Anna were swimming every day it seemed. They had a competitive travel team and, in the summer, there were outdoor summer leagues. There was a five-year stretch when I think the two of them swam as much as anyone in the county.

They were both pretty good. Ethan would go on to swim in high school, and his stroke was the backstroke. The breaststroke was absolutely not his event.

Which made that one summer even better. At these meets,

time passes before results start getting posted on the walls. Along with the times is the one asterisk that gets everyone's attention, "Regional Qualifier." This denotes that your time was fast enough to qualify for entry into the state regionals held in Raleigh.

As the officials posted the times for the thirteen-year-old boys breaststroke, a gasp went across the team and anyone nearby as they noticed there in big letters on the time sheet:

First place. Gold. Regional Qualifier. Ethan Brockman.

Some of the adults there knew it wasn't his time. Every swimmer kind of knew but wasn't sure. And Ethan—he definitely knew.

One of the parents leaned over and asked, "You're going to tell them, right? What will you do at the regionals in Raleigh?"

Ethan paused, grasping his medal, and after a quick thought with that pure look of early teenage innocence and mischief, he said boldly:

"No problem … I just retired from breaststroke."

He ended up not going to Raleigh to swim breaststroke at the regionals. And they didn't let him keep the medal. But he became quite the legend.

It was the perfect lesson tucked inside a kid's grin. Sometimes the win isn't the result. Sometimes the win is knowing exactly who you are.

FIELD NOTES
The Four Pillars of the Quiet Backbone

Over time and enough lived moments, the architecture reveals itself:

- Consistency

Kids don't need perfect. They need predictable.

- Non-reactivity

Your emotions don't chase theirs.

- Clean boundaries

You protect your peace without punishing their autonomy.

- Warmth with no invoice

Love with no expectation attached.

Put these four together and something profound happens:

- Kids relax into the relationship instead of performing inside it

When "Dad" Becomes "Pops"

Most men don't realize the moment they become the father their kids will remember. It isn't a big gesture. It's a seventeen-year-old boy walking into a room on your birthday, holding out a gift with a note, and casually dropping the word that rearranges something inside your chest.

"Hey, Pops."

You don't audition for that title. I had referred to myself in that manner over the years. "Hey, grab Pop's suitcase" or "Pop needs help moving the couch." But I didn't give any thought to it sticking. You don't negotiate something like that in a custody agreement. You don't earn it with lectures about respect and responsibility.

They give it to you. Kids inherit "Dad." Kids choose "Pops." And when they choose it, the whole relationship shifts just a notch to the side in a way you can't fully name.

Authority starts to feel like affection. Presence starts to feel like connection. Fatherhood starts to feel less like a job and more like companionship. On that birthday morning, Connor walked in, card in hand, grin half-hidden, and dropped it like it was nothing.

"Hey, Pops." It wasn't pride I felt. Pride is louder. It wasn't nostalgia either. That usually arrives later, on the drive home, when you're by yourself. What I felt was quieter and heavier at the same time.

Later, I looked at the note again and his handwriting, "Pops." No "Dad" scratched out. No correction. No testing it in pencil first. Just the new name, clean. That's when it hit me this wasn't a trial balloon. This was a coronation.

Pops didn't happen in my 1.0 nervous system—the over-explaining, over-texting, over-owning-every-feeling version. That version of me tried too hard and ran too hot. Kids don't crown that guy. They step carefully around him.

Pops happened after the frequency change. After I finally settled into a calmer version of myself. After my boys stopped having to manage my emotions and could just breathe around me. That's how kids talk when they don't have the language for "your nervous system finally feels safe to stand next to."

NOTES FROM A DIVORCED DAD
What to Carry Forward

- Guidance and control aren't the same thing
- Pressure can masquerade as protection
- Kids borrow your nervous system before they borrow your rules
- Trust grows where fear recedes
- The win is character, not compliance

PART V

THE WIDE
OPEN ROAD

Insight is great. It's also cheap. A man can have a head full of good ideas and still walk into his house like a storm cloud.

This part is where the work becomes repeatable. Not perfect. Repeatable. What you do when you're tired. What you do when you're provoked. What you do when your mood flips in two seconds. How you repair after you miss it—which you will, because you're human.

Practice is where fathers are made. Not the big vacations. Not the speeches in the car. The small moments that pile up: the way you respond when your kid is upset, the way you handle disrespect, the way you say no, the way you say you're sorry, the way you come back after you leave.

A lot of dads live in a pressure chamber. They want every minute with their kids to count, so they over-function. They over-teach. They make the room tight. And then they wonder why the kids don't relax. The truth is simple: kids relax around steadiness. Not around control.

This part turns Soft Eyes, Strong Spine into a daily posture. It's where you build a home inside yourself that your kids can feel. Not because you're always right. Because you're reliably regulated. Calm becomes the air they grow up breathing.

COMING HOME ON PURPOSE

Building a Life You Don't Have to Escape

An amazing thing started to happen as I went on this journey of true introspection—my frequency changed, my attunement changed, my emotional availability changed. And with it came the chance for real connections to take shape again. Not always one-on-one, but in a way that settled a room.

There's a kind of morning a man doesn't notice until he's lived long enough to recognize its weight. Not a holiday. Not a birthday. Not a day anyone else would circle on a calendar. Just a Tuesday. Or maybe a Wednesday. Something forgettable on paper.

But on this morning, the house feels different, quiet in a way that isn't empty, warm in a way that isn't staged. Sunlight hits the kitchen in a clean, unhurried way. My chest isn't buzzing. My shoulders aren't preparing for an invisible punch. My coffee tastes exactly like coffee. No more, no less.

I hear the refrigerator hum, a single floorboard creak, the

mug feels warm in my hand. Winter light hits the counters clean and honest. It's not a "new life" morning, just a real one. And for the first time in years, I am simply here.

Standing inside a life I didn't stumble into or endure my way toward, but a life I actually built. On purpose. One small, steady decision at a time.

There's no internal parade. Just a quiet truth settling inside me. *My life finally fits the man I'm becoming.*

That's the real meaning of coming home on purpose. Not reinvention. Not a comeback. Not a dramatic announcement of "New Eric." It's the slow alignment of your inner world with the outer one you're finally able to inhabit. 1.0 ran on fear. 2.0 runs on purpose.

And one ordinary morning, without any fanfare, you realize you're living from that place. Not talking about it, not intending to, not wishing for it, actually living it. When the inside finally matches the outside.

Your life didn't change in sweeping gestures. It changed in small adjustments only a man living inside them would notice. The counter got cleared not for guests, but for your mind. Not spotless, just clear enough to set your keys down without feeling behind. The counter becomes a surface again, not a scoreboard.

The porch lights went on timers not to impress anyone, but to make your home greet you too. That small click of control— lights on before you pull in—loosens something in your shoulders. You lit a candle when the kids weren't there not for ambience, but because the house finally felt like a place that deserved warmth. Cedar, vanilla, wood smoke, whatever it is, it's warmth you chose on a normal night, not something you had to earn.

Your playlists shifted from filling silence to creating atmosphere. Low volume. No performance. Just sound that makes the rooms feel inhabited. You walked into Planet Fitness like you belonged, Soft Eyes, steady gait, not performing confidence, but simply wearing it. Front desk beep, rubber mats, a few plates clanking, then your breath finding its own pace. You're not scanning. You're just there.

That's the surprising thing about coming home. You don't arrive with a spectacle. You just start recognizing yourself again. For the first time in years, your inner life and your outer life finally shook hands.

The Micro-Moments That Reveal You've Already Come Home

One evening at Home Depot, 5:30 p.m. The store quiet in that after-work lull. And there I am—moving without urgency, without tension. Grounded in my own pace. Unhurried. At ease in my own skin.

A body and a mind in the same moment. Concrete underfoot. Cool air. Distant beeps. Nothing profound, except you're not rushing like you're being chased.

The Airport Walk is the same way. North Face jacket. Phones in each pocket. Headphones. A stride without apology. People notice calm in a man before they ever name it. Women linger. Men adjust. Kids look without understanding why.

Same carpets. Same kiosks. The familiar airport smell. Only you're not narrating it. You move like a man who knows where he's going and doesn't need anyone to confirm it. You're not projecting confidence. You're emitting ease.

Shoulders down. Jaw loose. Eyes up, tuned not controlling.

Circle K stop with Connor "Hey, Pops..." Nothing inflated. Nothing stretched. Just a son talking to his dad on a random afternoon in a gas station parking lot. A moment that doesn't need to be more than it is.

Connor's voice comes through easy, like he doesn't have to manage you. 2.0 doesn't over-interpret. 2.0 simply receives.

Friday Night Vinyl

A quiet house. A record spinning. A kitchen that finally feels lived in. You feeling the week without drowning in any of it. Needle settles, a little crackle, then the room fills. Soft light, the kind of quiet that doesn't feel lonely.

None of these moments are dramatic. But together, they form a truth. I'm no longer surviving my life. I'm inhabiting it.

Music, aging, and the quiet recalibration. Music has always been one of my languages. I grew up on Springsteen, Clapton, the Stones, songs that made a suburban kid from Sharon feel connected to a world he hadn't lived yet.

Then the '90s. Pearl Jam on long drives, U2 on flights, Aerosmith when I needed edge without chaos.

Now, in my fifties, my playlists tell a different story. They aren't about escape. They aren't about filling space. They aren't keeping the loneliness away. They're about atmosphere. Building a life through sound. Creating moments instead of hiding inside them.

A track that fits the moment while I cook. Sound as permission to slow down and stay here.

The moment when Connor picked up the Black Keys ornament and quietly hung it on the Christmas tree wasn't about music at all. Ornament light in the hand, heavy in meaning, tree lights flickering in the glass as he hangs it without a speech.

It was a sentence in the language the two of us invented. It said, "I'm here. I feel this too. This is home."

A House That Finally Felt Like Yours

For years, Gastonia was just where I lived. Not homes—just a collection of addresses. Base camps. Emotionally, it felt like renting space inside someone else's life. Everything felt temporary in that divorced-dad way: kids in and out, custody cycles, the silence between weekends heavy enough to feel like responsibility. The newest house was nicer, but it never felt like it belonged to anyone.

But this year, something shifted—quietly. Not new furniture. A remodel of myself. The house became mine because I became someone who could live inside it.

Solo nights. I straightened the kitchen because it settled me. Lit the Christmas lights because they changed the feel of the room. Sat on the couch without my phone. Moved through the space like a man who finally belonged in his own life.

Things stayed consistent. The house held its temperature. Evenings unfolded without adjustment. Small rituals read like self-respect. And the kids felt it immediately. Connor moved with less tension. Owen's texts stayed warm. Ethan drifted closer without being pulled. Anna, after nine years, sent a small, real reply.

I didn't need to announce the change. They heard it in my voice—less edge, more room. Kids don't inherit rules. They inherit frequency. And mine had finally steadied.

FIELD NOTES
What Healing Actually Looks Like

Real healing isn't cinematic. It's doing fewer fear-based things than you used to and instead:

- Letting texts breathe
- Answering later instead of from panic
- Staying seated during conflict
- Accepting "K" from a kid as enough
- Going to bed instead of doom-scrolling
- Stepping out of old family patterns before they take the wheel
- Not disappearing; just calmer behavior and that's enough to change a life

Work: The External Storm You Didn't Let Inside

Coming home didn't happen because life got easy. Work was still chaotic—trade shows, leadership churn, corporate reshuffling, badge lanyards, hotel hallways that all smell the same, trade-show lights, carbon swatches in my bag, noise everywhere. Except in you. 1.0 would've treated every email as a referendum on your worth. 2.0 simply said, "I'm going to do my job, and I'm going to stop carrying what isn't mine."

My kids didn't know about org charts, margins, or shifting roles. They didn't need to. What they felt was simple. Dad wasn't vibrating anymore. Less pacing. Fewer sighs. More eye contact.

A dad whose body isn't telling a different story than his mouth. And that changed the temperature of the entire house.

The Back-Nine Realization

One evening, walking the sidewalk loop outside my house where usually not much happens, a thought surfaced in the calm. Unforced—the way thoughts do when a man finally stops fighting himself. Streetlights pooling on pavement. Cool air on my face. Shoes hitting in a steady rhythm. Movement as life, not escape.

The thought: *My next home might be Gaston Memorial.* It wasn't dark. It wasn't morbid. It wasn't even sad. It was honest. It was something I'd said before without thinking too hard, a way of skirting the fog I was in. At the time, it fit. In many ways I was playing out the string. Content to be on the "back nine of life," as the expression goes.

But that night, walking with the sting of honesty in my ribs, the words came back with weight. It's hard to explain, but like many things in this book, once you say it and really see it, you can't unsee it. I didn't feel fear, or pessimism, or cynicism—just acceptance.

And honesty, at any age, is freedom. The realization wasn't "I'm running out of time." It was "I'm not living the rest of my life the way I lived the first half." Not resignation. Resolution.

I realized that if this is home for the rest of my days, I'm finally going to live in it fully.

The Moment I Realized I Wasn't Escaping Anymore

It happened one quiet night at home, no kids around. The TV muted. Music low. The kitchen clean. My phone in my hand. The house breathing around me. And in that stillness, a thought surfaced—not dramatic, not emotional, just true. *For the first time in my life, I'm not trying to escape my own life.*

Not fantasizing. Not spiraling. Not in a fog. Not narrating my worth. Not running mental surveillance. Not rehearsing tomorrow's conversations. Just present. Awake. Unhurried. Inside my own life instead of running ahead of it. I didn't rebuild the house. I rebuilt the man living inside it.

NOTES FROM A DIVORCED DAD
What to Carry Forward

- Home is a frequency before it's a location
- Intention beats arrival
- You're allowed to inhabit your life, not just manage it
- Presence is how a man "comes home"
- The return is a choice you keep making

SOFT EYES, STRONG SPINE

Calm, Practiced Daily

At Planet Fitness, what I notice first is the lighting. Fluorescent. Relentless. A singles bar without the booze—and without the agreement that anyone is there to be social.

On paper, it's the least romantic place on earth: purple walls, spray bottles, TVs hanging everywhere, and that faint smell of Lysol and effort. The rubber-mat smell mixes with disinfectant, lockers clack open and shut, and the big NO JUDGMENT ZONE branding smiles at you like a dare.

But if you're a man who's slowly unclenched his nervous system, it becomes something else entirely. It becomes a lab. The gym may be one of the most honest rooms in America. Nobody can fake their frequency in there.

You can lie in your marriage, fake it at work, perform your way through a whole social life, but under fluorescent lights, with your body moving and your breath exposed, the truth shows up.

You can hear it in the breathing, in the small effort sounds—the body telling the truth while the mouth says he's "fine."

It becomes a quiet emotional health meter. It becomes one of the best places in the world to practice the code this whole book is built on.

Soft Eyes. Strong Spine. In the wild.
Not as a slogan. As a minute-by-minute choice.

I swipe in. The twenty-something at the desk gives me the same small nod I've been getting for months now. Not flirtatious, not overexcited. Just a "Hey, I know you. You're here. We're good." My shoulders are already lower than they would've been ten years ago.

Old wiring—The Tightened Life—would've had me scanning. "Who's here? Who's watching? Do I look out of place? Is the machine I like taken? Am I going to have to navigate somebody's energy?"

New wiring—the Strong Spine, calmer posture—lets me walk in with a different internal script. "Breathe. Find your lane. You're allowed to be here. No one needs anything from you. You don't need anything from them." Same room. Same people. Same fluorescent lights.

It is subtle but there is a shift. This is the reason I wrote the book. Not to go to Planet Fitness and feel more comfortable. But because when you start to see things you have never seen in thirty years, you can never unsee them. You have completely stepped out of the trees to see the forest.

After years of living out of tune, small connections begin to land differently. They feel real. Genuine. Like something you can finally trust.

A couple days earlier, Connor had looked at me over breakfast with one of those quiet half smiles he gives when he's reading my emotional weather. Nothing dramatic. Just a kid sensing his father isn't tightened the way he used to be. Connor was half in his breakfast and half in his own head, quiet, observant, catching that I wasn't running the old internal weather channel the whole time.

Soft Eyes don't just change how you see rooms. They change how the people who love you read your presence. Connor didn't have to say a word. That small smile was his way of saying, "You feel different, Pops." And the wild thing was, he was right. I take a slow breath and let the room come into focus. My jaw is loose. My shoulders relaxed. Same room. Different man.

Back at the gym, I'm back on the ellipticals—same row, same rhythm. I clock the familiar cohorts, the way you start to recognize regulars at a neighborhood diner:

- The Overachievers who stretch for eight minutes for a ten-minute workout
- The High School Crew with hoodies up and big energy
- The Treadmill Philosophers walking and solving their lives
- The Divorced Dad Comeback Squad quietly doing their laps
- The Quiet Killers who don't say a word

The place has its own soundtrack—treadmill thumps, a plate

clang that echoes once, somebody's breath getting honest on the last two reps. And then there's my cohort:

- The Dads Doing Their Second Draft—we're not here to impress anyone. We're just trying to outrun our cholesterol and our past decisions.

I've added a little muscle. Lost a little weight. But the thing that's changed isn't how I look. It's how I see.

Soft Eyes. Strong Spine. Right here. In the gym. In the most ordinary room in the world. And once a man understands that, the entire idea of "masculine change" stops being abstract and lands where it always should have lived: In the way he walks across a floor. In the way he looks at people. In the way his body finally catches up to what his mind has known for years.

What Soft Eyes Actually Mean

Most men imagine Soft Eyes and think weakness. Sadness. Neediness. Puppy-dog energy. Some kind of romantic, apologetic stare. That's not what we're talking about.

Soft Eyes are not:

- A plea
- An apology
- A performance
- A please-like-me gaze

Soft Eyes are not emotional softness, they are nervous system clarity. They signal to the world: "I am not here to take anything from you."

Soft Eyes are:

- Presence without urgency
- Awareness without agenda
- The look of a man who has nothing to prove, nothing to sell, and nothing to hide

Soft Eyes: What People Feel

Most men assume Soft Eyes is a metaphor. It isn't. It's physical, though not in a way you can manufacture.

You've felt this before. You're standing across from someone who isn't trying to win the moment, isn't scanning for advantage, isn't carrying an agenda in their face. The space feels calmer. You trust it without knowing why.

That isn't charisma. It's nervous-system posture showing up in the eyes. This isn't something you do. It's something that appears. When a man is tightened, the body quietly recruits the face:

- The brow tightens just enough to monitor
- The eyes narrow toward outcome
- The jaw holds a low, constant tension

It was the ongoing effort required to hold things together. People rarely name it, but they feel it as pressure correction, urgency, expectation.

When the tensing drops, the face stands down. The brow settles. The eyes take in more than one point at a time. The jaw loosens. Breath falls lower. The signal changes.

People feel presence without urgency. Attention without

agenda. Strength without armor. Soft Eyes aren't weakness. They don't come from collapsing or disengaging.

They come from a man whose spine is already doing its job so his face doesn't have to. This isn't about adjusting your expression. If you're trying to change your eyes, you've already missed it. Soft Eyes are what remain when you stop managing the moment and simply inhabit it.

Soft Eyes say, "I'm here. I see the room. I'm not tightened against it."

You feel it in your face first:

- Less squinting
- Less micro-contracting around the eyes
- Less scanning for what might go wrong

You feel it next in your throat:

- The tightness easing
- The swallow coming easier
- The voice a half-octave lower

Then, eventually, you feel it in your chest.

The space that used to be filled with tension, anticipation, self-protection, and hypervigilance finally has some room in it. That's what other people are responding to when they look back. Not perfection. Not looks. Not bravado.

Calm.

They're reading your frequency. They're reading whether you are safe to be around. Soft Eyes broadcast that safety long before your words ever get a chance.

What Is Strong Spine

If Soft Eyes are the broadcast, Strong Spine is the signal underneath.

Strong Spine is not swagger. It's not domination, or "alpha," or pounding your chest.

Strong Spine:

- Strong Spine is what keeps a man from collapsing into other people's moods
- It is the quiet internal sentence that says "I do not leave myself to manage you"
- You know where you stand
- You know what you will and won't tolerate
- You can feel your feet on the ground in hard conversations
- You can say "no" without explaining it five different ways

Strong Spine is the thing that keeps you from folding, not the thing that makes you rigid. It lets you stay soft in your gaze because you're not in danger of collapsing in your posture. You don't need to puff up. You don't need to shrink. You don't need to posture either. You can just be a man in his actual size.

In a gym, that looks like this: You take the elliptical you like, without apologizing for existing. You move when you're done, not thirty seconds early because someone walked up behind you and now you feel guilty. You wipe your machine, nod, and walk out.

In life, it looks like this: When your ex's energy spikes, your body doesn't automatically match it. When a kid rolls their eyes, you don't read it as a verdict on your worth as a father. When a client comes in hot, you don't join their storm. You stay steady and let them cool against your calm.

Strong Spine is the quiet, internal sentence that lives underneath all of that. *I am allowed to be here as I am. I don't have to perform to belong.* Soft Eyes keep you open. Strong Spine keeps you from disappearing. Together, they're a way of living, not a slogan. Soft Eyes without Strong Spine collapses into passivity. Strong Spine without Soft Eyes hardens into pressure.

The magic happens when they live together in one man. They're an operating system with warmth and boundaries.

FIELD NOTES

The Three Movements Inside a Man

The Tightened Life:
You live like a human airbag, always ready,
always tense, always convinced the next impact is
your job to absorb. You mistake vigilance for love
and exhaustion for devotion.

Strong Spine / Awakening:
You start noticing your body changing before
your life does. Your breath deepens. Your
shoulders lower. You stop gripping every
conversation like a negotiation. Calm stops being
an accident and starts becoming a skill.

The Wide Open Road Ahead:

You no longer have to think about this stuff. It's baked into you. Your nervous system finally feels like home. Ordinary rooms become the place you prove nothing and live fully.

The Emotional Health Meter

Every man has an emotional battery—whether he realizes it or not. In the years of divorce fog and carrying everything for everyone, mine stayed in low-power mode. Think single digits on a power meter.

Every negative conversation costs something. So does every moment with your kids that feels loaded. And every drive home from work spent quietly tallying what could still come apart.

Each moment chips away at your charge. You don't notice at first. But over time, it changes how you show up in rooms.

At 10%, you don't make eye contact.

At 5%, you don't stay engaged in conversations.

At 1%, you're not even really walking into rooms—you're just passing through them on the way to the next obligation.

But not every moment takes. Some give. That's why the smallest interactions start to matter more than they should— tiny moments that pass between people without effort or agenda. Micro-connections. A nod. A shared joke. Someone remembering your name.

They don't fully recharge the battery. But they add just enough to keep you going. They slow the drain. And some days, that's everything.

What the real world gave me wasn't just the daily errands. It gave me *micro-charges*. Tiny, ordinary, human moments that refilled the battery I didn't even know I'd drained.

The nod from the front-desk kid. A soft glance from the corporate woman who clocks that you look pulled together. The older regular at the grocery store who looks like someone's granddad and gives you that warm, approving look that says "we're both still in the game." The quiet head tilt from a casual encounter at the hotel bar.

None of these are pickup moments. None of these are "moves." They're micro-connections. And micro-connections, for a man walking out of the Tightened Life, are emotional recharging. Not in some dramatic movie-montage way. In a realistic "I just need to feel human again" way.

After a while, your meter moves from low single digits to 55%, to 88% or higher. Your drive home starts to feel different. Not high. Not hungry for attention. Just steadier.

You notice the sky again. You turn the radio up a notch. Your mind isn't running ahead or circling old ground. You're just a man in a car who got a solid workout and shared space with a few other humans, each carrying their own lives. That's healing.

Most men aren't emotionally unavailable. They're emotionally undercharged. A starving man looks disengaged, but he's just out of power.

Soft Eyes let you see those moments.

Strong Spine keeps you from chasing them.

You don't go to the gym to get validated. You go to be yourself. The validation is a side effect of a nervous system that's finally running on a calmer operating system.

Micro–Physical Improvements

I want to be careful here. There's a lot written about the connection between mental health and physical health, and most of it gets fuzzy fast. The correlations are hard to prove. The variables are messy.

People want clean lines where there usually aren't any. So this isn't a claim. It's an observation.

During the stretch of time this book was coming into focus, my physical health improved. Not in a dramatic, before-and-after way. Quietly. Gradually. Almost incidentally.

Some of it is easy to account for. I ate better. I spent more time in the gym. I slept more consistently. Those things matter, and I'm not pretending otherwise. But something else shifted too.

My weight came down—almost thirty pounds since I started writing this. My sleep got deeper. The tinnitus that had been a steady presence for years softened to the margins. The joints that have carried the cost of back surgeries at fifty-seven felt less swollen, less inflamed, more usable.

I don't know how much of that is mental clarity and how much is behavior change. I don't know where one ends and the other begins. I only know they seemed to move together.

What I do know is that when my internal state became more regulated, my body felt less like it was locking all the time. Less clenched. Less on alert. I wasn't trying to fix my health by thinking better thoughts. I was just living with less background tension—and my body responded in ways I didn't predict or chase.

This isn't advice. It's not a formula. It's not a promise. It's simply what happened when I stopped living at a constant low-grade strain and started carrying myself differently through the day. Softer eyes. A stronger spine. Fewer internal alarms ringing at once. Whatever the mechanism, the outcome was real. And it reminded me that the body keeps its own ledger. Sometimes, when the noise quiets and the posture changes, it adjusts the numbers on its own

FIELD NOTES
The Micro-Charge Rules

A caveat on all these micro-observations—
if you're going to use any public space as an
emotional health lab, you need guardrails. Here's
the code I live by:

You can observe behavior, but you can't assign
meaning:
You're allowed to notice who glances over, who
tends to arrive when you do, who nods, who
drifts closer to your row of machines. Those are
facts. What you're not allowed to do is build a
story out of them. No fantasies, no assumptions,
no "maybe she's into me." Observation without
story keeps your frequency clean.

Default to the least dramatic explanation:
If a woman walks by you three times, the most
likely answer is: that's the path she walks. Period.
Calm men choose the explanation that doesn't
inflate their ego or their anxiety. "She's here to

work out" is almost always true. This is where that old *Men Are from Mars…* idea finally turns practical: 1.0 turns a harmless micro-charge into a finish-line fantasy; 2.0 lets it be what it is and keeps walking clean.

Never measure yourself against anyone in the room:
You're not competing with the twenty-three-year-old benching his body weight. You're not auditioning for anyone. Your lane is your breath, your machine, your towel, your exit. That's it.

A change in someone else's behavior is not a message to you:
She switched to a different machine. He stopped nodding. They started talking closer to the free weights. None of that is your business. 2.0 men don't spend their bandwidth decoding mysteries that were never theirs to solve.

The only frequency you govern is your own:
You don't control who looks, who doesn't, who seems open, who seems closed. You control your posture, your pace, your breath, and your presence. That's more than enough work for one man.

Awareness without agenda is the superpower:
You're allowed to see everything. You're not
allowed to reach for everything. Women, men,
kids, strangers, they all feel the difference
between a man who is present and a man who
is hungry. There are a thousand small, clean
pleasures in a day—eyes meeting, a nod, a wave,
a moment of warmth—and none of them require
you to turn it into a story.

Follow those rules and the places you go stop
being ego arenas.

They become places to practice being steady in
the wild.
Soft Eyes, Strong Spine. No story. Just presence..

How the Code Changes Rooms

Here's how it shows up in real time. Soft Eyes open the room. Strong Spine holds it steady. At home. The refrigerator humming. The kitchen settles.

The old me walked into the kitchen tightened, braced for what might be waiting. The new me walks in, takes a breath, and actually sees my kids. I notice Connor's face before his grades. I answer with presence instead of preloaded speeches.

Soft Eyes: you're actually looking.

Strong Spine: you're not collapsing when the energy isn't perfect.

Ex-wife. There was a time when any text from the kids' mom hit my system like an alarm. I'd read it three times, hear a tone I couldn't prove, and start building a response like I was walking into a fight. Now I treat it like information.

I read it once. I respond to what's being asked. I don't litigate history through an iMessage thread.

Soft Eyes: you see the actual words.

Strong Spine: you refuse to step into the old emotional courtroom.

College choices. Moving out. Relationships you're not sure about. The Tightened Life dad manages from anxiety. He fills the space with advice, warnings, and reassurance, all framed as "just wanting what's best." The Strong Spine dad asks good questions, listens, and then says, "I trust you," even when his stomach flips.

Soft Eyes: you see the young adult, not just the child.

Strong Spine: you hold your boundary without making their life your scoreboard.

Kids don't need perfect fathers; they need fathers whose eyes don't disappear and whose spine doesn't collapse.

In public. A cashier hands you change with a rushed expression, and instead of matching her tension, you meet her eyes for a half second with soft presence. No fixing, no performance, just human acknowledgment. And the world softens back.

Grocery stores. School auditoriums. Airport gates. The places that once kept you on edge now register as they are. You're still yourself—sarcasm, dad jokes, a heart that stays engaged—but the baseline isn't anticipation of trouble. It's readiness.

Soft Eyes: you notice small kindnesses you used to miss.
Strong Spine: you're not knocked over by other people's noise.

I notice it on New Hope Road driving past the construction, where I can see the clearing now and the trees thin out and the sky opens just enough to remind me I'm not carrying the world alone anymore. I used to grip the wheel the whole way, running conversations ahead of time, bracing for whatever came next.

Now the road feels wider. Same asphalt. Same commute. Different posture behind the wheel. This is what life looks like when your body finally matches the wisdom your mind has been learning. It doesn't arrive loudly. It just holds. It's a thousand small, ordinary moments where you are simply a steady man moving through his life with less trepidation.

FIELD NOTES

How You Know Your Body Has Caught Up

You don't realize you've changed in real time.
You notice it sideways.

- You get home from work and your first instinct isn't to reach for your phone
- Your kid texts you a meme instead of a crisis
- You sit in the car for an extra minute, not because you're hiding, but because the quiet actually feels good
- Your ex calls and your pulse doesn't jump thirty beats

These are the nervous system's way of tapping you on the shoulder and saying:

- "We're okay now"
- "We're not in danger"
- "You can live here"

From Practice to Posture

Soft Eyes, Strong Spine starts as practice. You'll think about it consciously at first. "Okay, soften the face. Drop the shoulders. Breathe. Don't over-explain. Just say the thing clearly."

You'll bring it into restaurants, your kitchen at home, and co-parenting meetings—like a checklist running quietly in the background. That's fine. There's no shame in practice.

Over time, though, something better happens. It stops being a concept and starts being a posture. You don't have to remind yourself to soften. You just do. You don't have to steel yourself for every conversation. You just show up.

At some point the code stops being something you practice and becomes something the people around you trust. And trust is what changes everything. You don't have to rehearse every possible outcome. You just trust that the version of you who walks into that room will be able to handle what comes.

That's the moment the idea drops into your body. Nothing around you has changed. Same bills. Same kids. Same history. Same ex. Same work. But you're meeting it from a different place.

The man who is awake, who is steady, he can walk into a fluorescent gym, a tense kitchen, a hard meeting, or a bleacher full of complicated family history and still feel his feet on the ground.

Soft Eyes.
Strong Spine.
Same life.
Different way of inhabiting it.

And without even noticing it happen, you start living closer to the version of yourself who walks the Wide Open Road, not someday, not in theory, but right now, inside the ordinary minutes of your life. You don't force it. You don't chase it. You just grow into it.

NOTES FROM A DIVORCED DAD
What to Carry Forward

- Soft Eyes are the signal: "You're safe with me"

- Strong Spine is the vow: "I won't abandon myself"
- Softness without spine collapses, spine without softness isolates
- Together, they create a man people can trust
- This isn't a concept, it's a posture, its an operating system

STRONG SPINE IN THE REAL WORLD

Holding the Line Without Hardening

The old wiring said, "If you see everything coming, nothing can hurt the people you love." But life isn't a hurricane you can outguess. And love isn't measured in how tightly you grip. The new lens provided a quieter reaction. A steadier breath. A conversation I didn't force. A silence that didn't scare me. A decision I didn't over-explain.

It arrived in places I'd walked through a thousand times—kitchens, airports, the aisles of Planet Fitness, the cold rental car row in Detroit—but now, finally, without the old familiar narrowing in my chest.

That's how a man knows he's changed. Not because people tell him. Not because he gives himself credit. But because life hands him back the same thresholds that once shook him, and this time his body responds with something new. Nothing flinches. There's a deep, masculine humility in that realization.

And eventually, the people around him feel the shift long before they can articulate it. Kids feel it. Coworkers feel it. Even strangers at the gym sense something different in the way he moves: unhurried, unclenched, carrying his own center without needing to borrow anyone else's.

You don't become a different man overnight. You become him one untightened moment at a time.

Moving Through the World Differently

One of the early times I noticed the shift was a conversation with one of my kids. It wasn't even at any of the places mentioned before that I had started to see the shift. It was in my own hallway.

Late at night, the house quiet, dishes done, everyone else tucked into their own worlds. For most of my adult life, that was a dangerous hour. The moment between responsibility and rest. The time of day when men think too much.

I walked down the hallway, lights low, just going to brush my teeth … and realized something astonishing. My shoulders were down. Not forced down. Not corrected. Just naturally, comfortably low. If your whole life has been built on vigilance, you know what that means. A lowered shoulder is not just posture, it's permission. It's the nervous system saying you don't have to carry the whole house anymore.

I didn't celebrate it. Didn't text anyone. Didn't even smile. I just noticed. And noticing is always the beginning of embodiment.

The Car Test

A car used to be the loudest place in my life, the cockpit of worry, the command center for overthinking. For years, every drive became a silent debrief. *What's coming next? What haven't I fixed? What will fall if I stop trying?*

After 1.0 collapses, men often think the goal is to eliminate these thoughts. But the real breakthrough is when those thoughts don't require management. One morning driving to the airport, I realized I was doing something I never used to do: Nothing.

I wasn't replaying conversations. I wasn't running simulations. I wasn't stiffening my stomach to prepare for something that might never happen. I was just driving. The road was the road.

My hands were on the wheel. My breath was slow and normal. And in that moment, I understood something men rarely say out loud. Peace feels ordinary. Ordinary breath. Ordinary drive. Ordinary body. Ordinary day. That's the miracle men keep missing, the miracle sitting right there in the mundane.

The "Not Needing to Announce Anything" Test

There's a strange thing that happens when a man changes. He stops trying to prove that he's changed. He doesn't need to pitch it to a new partner. Doesn't need to sell it to his ex. Doesn't need to manage his kids' reaction. Doesn't need coworkers to validate that he's more grounded now. He can let it be true without applause.

A man with a Strong Spine doesn't make speeches about his spine. He lives from it. And the steadiness does what it does—

people feel it. The room organizes around it without force, without pressure, without demand.

That's one of the quiet gifts of 2.0: You stop hunting for verification. You trust yourself enough to let the world catch up or not. Either way, you're not bending. And here's the part that matters—this book isn't an announcement. It's a record.

Months into 2.0, I noticed I wasn't absorbing other people's moods anymore. I wasn't studying them. I wasn't calibrating myself against every sigh, every shift in tone, every micro-expression. It sounds small. It isn't. It's seismic.

For a man who learned to be the stabilizer in his marriage, and became the quiet buffer in his adult life, not absorbing was a revolution. It meant I could stay steady without managing the entire emotional field. It meant I could be in a room without becoming the room. It meant I could let other people have their storms without believing they were mine to solve. A Strong Spine is not rigidity. It's containment. It's being exactly where you are, without leaking into everyone else's weather.

At some point, and I don't know when, I stopped raising my shoulders to meet the world, and the world didn't collapse. That's the moment every man needs to discover. Nothing falls apart when you stop gripping. People don't abandon you. Your kids don't withdraw. Your relationships don't weaken. Your competence doesn't evaporate. Your masculinity doesn't dull. Your authority doesn't slip. What falls away is only the fear. And underneath it is the posture you were supposed to have your entire life:

Soft Eyes. Strong Spine.

Calm presence. Steady center.

A steady body. Clear attention.

A man standing in the life he built—not as its brake, but as its anchor.

Strong Spine at Work (Where 1.0 Used to Live)

Most men don't fall apart at home. They fall apart at work. Not visibly. Not theatrically. Not in a way anyone could point to. Men fall apart internally in the gap between who they are and who they think they're supposed to be.

Work was always where my 1.0 wiring hid best. It rewarded the over-functioning. It praised the vigilance. It benefited from the scanning. And for years, it fed off my belief that my value came from carrying too much. Aerospace and defense sales is not for the faint of heart.

The cycles are long. The stakes are high. The problems are technical. The timelines are unpredictable. The customers are demanding in a way only aerospace engineers can be—precise, unyielding, certain. 1.0 thrived in that pressure because pressure was his native language.

But 2.0 doesn't operate that way. 2.0 doesn't tighten. 2.0 doesn't sprint internally. 2.0 doesn't confuse motion with importance. 2.0 doesn't mistake urgency for meaning. 2.0 walks into a meeting and sees people, not threats. He hears questions, not tests. He feels tension, not danger. A Strong Spine changes not only how you respond to pressure ... it changes how pressure responds to you.

There was a morning outside of Dallas in a standard large Texas office park with a mix of manufacturing space and offices. A customer issue was unfolding, the kind that used to spike my heart rate before I even knew the details. 1.0 would've apologized before understanding anything, overexplained, sprinted emotionally to get ahead of the problem, burned energy trying to fix something that may not have been broken yet.

But 2.0 did something unheard of in my old operating system. He waited. Not passively. Not lazily. Not out of disengagement. He waited because calm men don't chase storms. They stand still long enough to see the real size of the cloud.

And the real cloud? Much smaller than my imagination had always made it. We solved the issue in twenty minutes. I didn't grip. Didn't tighten. Didn't sprint. I just … handled it.

And afterward, instead of the old internal shakiness, that adrenaline hangover men know too well, I felt nothing but a quiet return to center.

That's when I realized something essential. Strong Spine is not about dominance. It's about the absence of panic.

The Demotion That Became a Promotion

What was I thinking? On paper, it looked like I'd stepped backward. Back to my old title. Less authority. Less money. The kind of move men are trained to avoid because it bruises the ego, dents the wallet, and confuses the resume. But in real life, it felt like my body unclenched.

Here's the clean truth without the corporate details. I'd been asked to operate in a role that required me to "manage" outcomes I didn't actually control and to do it while still being tied to the same old dependencies that made the job impossible to do cleanly.

The structure was misaligned. The expectations were foggy. And the only way to succeed inside it was to live braced for impact. Always monitoring, always anticipating, always carrying pressure that didn't belong to me.

That version of work fits 1.0 perfectly. 1.0 thinks pressure is proof. 1.0 treats stress like a mortgage payment: *This is just what you owe if you want to be a man.* And for a while, I did what I've always done in my career—I out-prepared, out-worked, out-absorbed. I told myself I could muscle my way through it with competence and sheer will.

But then something shifted. Not in the company. In me. One night after about a year and a half in the new role and a long day of travel, rental cars, airports, the whole sales-life parade, I had the simplest thought: *What if I could put the toothpaste back in the tube? Would it be possible to actually ask to start things over again?*

What if I stopped trying to win a game that wasn't set up to be won? Not in a dramatic, quit-your-job way. In a strong-spine way. What if I asked to return to the work I'm actually built for? The work where I can create value without living inside other people's pressure. The position where I can do what I do best, keep my relationships clean, and go home with a nervous system that still belongs to me.

So I wrote a carefully worded email to my manager. We already had a meeting planned for that following Monday morning, and I asked her if we could also discuss my role.

The email wasn't an angry one. Not a grand declaration. A careful, respectful note that said I wanted to step back into business development. I wanted the roles to match reality. I wanted to do my job well and do it in a way that's sustainable.

Then I sent it … and went back to work. That's the part that still surprises me. Old me would've paced the house, refreshed his inbox, rehearsed arguments, tried to pre-manage everyone's reaction.

2.0 sent the message and didn't chase the echo. There was pushback. There was discomfort. There was a moment when I genuinely didn't know if I'd just talked myself into being replaced. But I kept doing my job calmly, steadily, and let the chips land where they were going to land.

When the decision came, it came quietly. A short Teams call, a simple reset of title and pay, and a return to a lane that fit. No victory lap. No revenge arc. Just a man choosing alignment over appearance.

And here's why it became a "promotion" in the only way that matters. I got my evenings back. I got my sleep back. I get to end the day, close the laptop, and not bring a storm home to my kids because my nervous system was still stuck in a boardroom that didn't exist.

Strong Spine isn't always standing taller. Sometimes it's stepping out of what's making you smaller and refusing to pretend you're fine just because the title says you should be.

FIELD NOTES
Honey Badger Mode

A Reset for the workday:
The honey badger is a fearless solitary animal
with many survival instincts.

Honey Badger Mode at your job:

It is not angry or disengaged.

It is focused on the work that's actually yours to

do, and lets the rest of the chaos roll off your fur.

Honey Badger Mode:

- Today, my only job is to do my job
- I'm not here to fix the company, win arguments, or read people's moods
- I work with others, not for their approval
- My focus: my accounts, my follow-ups, my results, that's it
- The management team runs the show—I don't need to care how or why
- The other sales reps do their thing—I'll do mine
- I protect my energy, I don't absorb their tension, gossip, or confusion
- I stay calm, steady, and professional—the kind of person who gets things done and goes home clean

Strong Spine Alone

A man can fool the world. He can even fool his family for a time. But he can never fool himself when he is alone.

This is the real test of a Strong Spine. Not how you carry yourself in the company of others, but how you carry yourself when the room is empty, the door clicks shut behind you, and no one is there to witness the posture you choose. The world believes men unravel alone. And some do.

But for the man who has recalibrated his emotional frequency, solitude becomes something deeper. A quiet measurement of calm. A private inventory of peace. A mirror with no distortions.

For me, that inventory showed up most clearly in unfamiliar rooms and unstructured time. Each one peeled back a different layer of what a Strong Spine actually feels like in the real world.

When I was on my own, away from routine, that's where the list told the truth. Not heroic. Not polished. Just a man, some quiet, and the realization that a lot of my exhaustion wasn't life at all. It was my habits.

I opened my notes app and started typing. There it was. The Fuck-It List. Not a bucket list, but a boundary list. I added a line that didn't need debate: Stop rehearsing conversations that haven't happened.

A Note from the Road–The Eric Fuck-It List

People tell you about their bucket lists all the time: Grand Canyon. Tuscany. Jump out of a plane. Kiss someone you love on a dock at sunset.

My list came later, and it pointed the other way. Not what I wanted to add before I died—what I was finally willing to subtract so I could live.

The Fuck-It List is where I park the things I'm done carrying. Not out of anger. Out of accuracy. It's not a manifesto. It's a private note that keeps my nervous system from volunteering for jobs it never applied for. On the list, I put things like:

- Staying in conversations past the moment they turn into performance
- Pretending I'm fine in rooms that cost me my peace
- Answering texts I don't owe answers to
- Trying to be liked by people who don't even like themselves

One line sits at the top like a header and a reminder: Protect your energy. Go home clean.

FIELD NOTES
The Fuck-It List (Not Anger, Clarity)

This is about seeing straight.

I'm not burning bridges—I'm stopping the pointless negotiations.

Clarity first. Then connection.

Open a note on your phone and title it

Fuck-It List.

Type: Protect your energy. Go home clean.

Then do three passes:

Pass 1 – Small stuff (easy wins):

- The apps that spike you
- The foods that fog you
- The habits that steal your mornings
- The airports, routes, routines that always drain you more than they're worth

Pass 2 – Social stuff (where you leak energy):

- Group texts you don't enjoy
- Conversations you stay in out of politeness
- Explaining yourself to people committed to misunderstanding you
- Being the "nice guy" in rooms that reward clarity, not niceness

Pass 3 – Deep stuff (where you perform):

- Emotional babysitting
- Proving you're okay
- Chasing a clean ending with people who need mess
- Rehearsing, pre-managing, forecasting storms

Keep it private. Keep it honest. Adjust as you go.
This isn't about not caring. It's about caring on purpose.

And somewhere in the middle of writing, if you're paying attention, you'll feel it. Something softens, something unclenches.
Your frequency returns to baseline.
Not to make your life bigger. Not to make your life smaller.
To make your life yours.

The Sales Call Where I Didn't Try to Save the Moment

My life isn't conference rooms and whiteboards. It's airports, customer sites, plant tours, safety glasses, and that strange little rhythm of walking into a lobby like you've been there a hundred times even when you haven't. And in sales, there's a specific kind of silence in a new prospect meeting that can make a man start tap-dancing internally.

You ask a question. You make a point. And then … the customer goes quiet. Old me leaned in right there. Soften the air. Make sure nobody feels tension, especially me. But this version of me didn't move. I let the pause sit where it belonged. Not as a tactic. Not as a "power move." Just … calm.

And after a few seconds, the customer said what needed to be said—the real objection, the real constraint, the real truth underneath the polite layer. It hit me later, in the rental car, that I'd finally stopped doing that old job. Trying to manage the whole room with my nervous system.

The Line That Landed Harder Than Praise

The new role had tightened me. For eighteen months or so, I was difficult to work with—over-managing, overcorrecting, bringing tension into rooms. When I chose to step back, the work fit better, and the company kept moving without issue. I wasn't perfect, but I was easier. A couple months after things settled, someone said something that stopped me—not because it was dramatic, but because it was unfamiliar.

"You're easy to work with."

In thirty-five years of working in sales, I'd gotten a few compliments along the way—"great job on that project, that was a huge win"—but nothing like this. This was a first. Easy. That's what Strong Spine looks like from the outside. Not intimidating. Not anxious. Not hovering. Not reactive. Just steady.

And that day, being called "easy" mattered more than being called impressive.

Strong Spine at Home

Work can be demanding. Fatherhood is different. It asks for steadiness, because kids don't just hear what you say—they feel how you're being.

They don't listen to your explanations. They don't care about your intentions. They feel your nervous system. Things like using the car, adjusting an allowance, or restricting a night out with a time limit are often the most important thing in your kid's life at that moment.

Strong Spine in fatherhood isn't sternness. It isn't control. It isn't "being the man of the house." It's quieter than that. It's the posture that says "I'm here. I'm steady. You don't need to manage me."

When a father has emotional availability, they sit closer. They talk longer. They don't measure every word like it's going to be graded. They relax.

That's the gift. Not answers. Not speeches. Not perfection. Presence your kids can lean against without thinking.

A Boundary Without Hardening

Not long after, one of the boys asked to take the car. It was framed as a question, but it carried weight. A time. A plan. The familiar pull to manage the reaction.

The old pattern would've kicked in—explaining, bargaining, staying ahead of the fallout. Instead, I stayed put. Present.

"No," I said. One syllable. Clean. The reasons were there, steady and unspoken. His face tightened, then released—a flicker of heat, a shrug that said he didn't care. The doorway held the pause.

I didn't chase him with a sermon. I didn't punish him with silence. I held the line and kept the room warm. "I know you don't like it," I said. "I'm still here." He walked off. Not a slam. Not peace either.

Just that teenage weather where the pressure drops and you feel it in the air. Later—after the dishes, after the house settled—I passed his room and knocked once. Not dramatic. Not apologizing for the boundary.

"You good?" I asked. A pause.

Then: "Yeah."

"Alright," I said. "Love you." And I meant it in the same tone as the no. That's repair. Not retreat. Connection without surrender.

Here's the truth no one tells men: Your kids don't need the strongest version of you. They need the calmest one. They need your breath, not your analysis; your steadiness, not your solutions, your presence, not your performance.

When a father carries a strong spine, he becomes shelter instead of weather. A place his kids can return to even after long winters, because his presence doesn't spike with need or collapse under fear. Strong Spine isn't power. It's the gift that lets everyone else exhale.

The Hotel Room: Where a Man Meets His True Frequency

A hotel room reveals everything about a man. Not the curated version. Not the polished version. Not the performance. The truth. I spend a lot of time in hotels. Maybe even more than planes and airports. Lifetime Marriott Platinum.

For most of my life, hotel rooms were pressure cookers. Too quiet. Too still. Too reflective. I'd leave the TV on in the background—noise, voices, anything to keep the room from getting too honest.

A man without peace can't sit in a quiet hotel room for ten minutes without feeling the hum of unfinished business, inner tension, and invisible expectations. But in 2.0? I began to feel something new. Nothing.

No dread. No churn.
No forced productivity. No pacing.
No fear of being alone with my own pulse.

Just a room. Just a bed. Just a man sitting with himself and feeling fine. That's when it hit. A man's strength isn't measured by how well he handles conflict or work or chaos. It's measured by how well he handles stillness.

And in that stillness, I noticed micro-movements. My breath was even. My shoulders stayed low. My jaw wasn't clenched.

My stomach wasn't tight. The evening didn't feel like a threat. I wasn't waiting for the next thing. I wasn't rehearsing tomorrow. I wasn't carrying anyone else's emotional weight. I was just there.

Men underestimate this state, but it is the foundation of a Strong Spine. Being alone without feeling lonely.

The Escalator at Detroit Airport
(The Moment the Body Proved the Mind Right)

I'm back at Detroit Metro (DTW) at the big escalator near the rental shuttle drop-off. I've stood here a lot. This is one of those places that reliably wakes up the loss-of-control vertigo I mentioned earlier.

It's a familiar misfire in my wiring. It shows up when I feel boxed in—limited options, nowhere to step out, no ability to make it better if it goes sideways. Standing here, the whole pattern clicks into place.

The building isn't cozy. It's a glass box with a pulse. Wet concrete outside. A grid of windows. And then the escalator—rising like a silver spine into the dark—under a sign in big letters: "Bridge to Terminal."

I used to read that sign like a warning. Not because the words were scary. Because I knew what waited on the other side.

Every man has a private battlefield. A place where his nervous system once betrayed him. A threshold that stored the old fear, the old wiring, the old story he carried for years. For me, that place was the escalator at DTW's Evans Terminal.

If you've never been there, when you get dropped off from the rental car busses, there is this massive escalator inside. I have traveled many airports across the country and the world, and this has to be one of the highest, longest escalators made.

Imagine a structure so tall it feels designed to measure your inner steadiness. A moving staircase that rises into a cathedral of glass and steel, narrowing your field of vision as it climbs. You step on, and for a moment it feels like a test.

Are you the man who grips the handrail or the man who trusts the ascent? For years, I was the first man. The gripper. The white-knuckler. The one whose stomach tightened as the ground fell away beneath him. The one who held the rail like a rope over a canyon, convinced one wobble could send everything crashing.

I hated that escalator. I feared it. And for some reason I never took the elevator. I always got on that escalator and expected a different outcome. And when I didn't get one, I faked normalcy with a performative calm that fooled no one, least of all myself. It wasn't the height. It wasn't the movement. It wasn't the machinery.

It was the story my nervous system told me. *You're not safe. You're not steady. You're one slip away from disaster, and there's no one to save you.* That's what fear does to a man. It convinces him he's always an inch away from collapse, even in places engineered for stability.

But then came the day everything changed. Not because I decided to conquer anything. Not because I psyched myself up. Not because I used coping mechanisms. It changed because my body finally, mercifully, caught up to the man I had become.

I rolled my suitcase across the wet pavement and walked toward the doors I'd walked through a hundred times. The wheels clicked through the sidewalk seams and skimmed the thin film of rainwater like it was trying to remember every trip. The sign was the same, "Bridge to Terminal."

With the beads of rain catching the light as the doors slid apart, it hit me. Oh … right. This is the place. This is the place that used to test me. This is the place that remembered my old posture. This is the place where 1.0 felt small. And without hesitation, without a single preparatory breath, I stepped onto the escalator.

Halfway up, I realized something impossible. My hands were in my pockets. I wasn't gripping. I wasn't leaning. I wasn't checking the rails. I wasn't scanning for the emergency stop button. I wasn't holding my breath. I wasn't running simulations of collapse.

Somewhere around that midpoint, I glanced down through the glass and saw the drop for what it was—long, clean, indifferent. People moved below like slow pieces on a board.

In the old wiring, that view would've been a trigger. This morning it was just height. Just geometry. I looked down through the glass—same drop, different body. My breath steady. My shoulders loose. It was simply height. I was bored. The body that once panicked now stood there, relaxed and casual. Unbothered.

I could've closed my eyes, I was so relaxed. I reached into my pocket and did something I could have never thought about before. Grabbed my phone and took some photos. There I was, midway up this once ominous escalator, hands in pockets, spine steady and frequency clean.

A man in a navy suit stood a few steps ahead of me, doing the old move I knew by heart. Feet planted wide. One hand welded to the rail. Trying to keep your front half from separating from your lower half. Shoulder tilted in like he believed the whole mechanism might buck him off. I could feel his story before he said a word.

He was gripping things in his life that had nothing to do with escalators. The mortgage. The pressures. The expectations. The quiet fear that if anything went wrong, he would be the one who failed the people he loves.

And here's the part I didn't expect: I didn't look at him with superiority. I looked at him with recognition. Soft Eyes. Like, "Yeah. I know that grip." I wasn't only rooting for his safe ascent; I was also silently rooting for the moment he stopped treating stability like it's fragile.

That used to be me. And for a brief moment, an old echo stirred in my chest, the faintest shadow of the man I used to be. Just enough for contrast. Just enough to see the distance I'd traveled. Then a thought landed, clean and unforced. You're already across. Not the escalator—the internal bridge. The one I'd been trying to cross for decades.

It was the version of me made of the old wiring, inherited vigilance, and the belief that my safety depended on never letting go. Standing there, hands in pockets, rising with the machine, I understood something I'd never felt in my bones before: This isn't a victory. This is alignment. The escalator wasn't the test. It was the mirror. It was showing me the man I had become without fanfare, without ceremony, without needing anyone to witness it.

When the escalator reached the summit, I stepped off with no hop, no wobble, no quick recalibration of my feet. Just a clean transfer of weight from moving stairs to solid floor. A simple moment. An ordinary moment. But, also, the physical proof that the internal wiring had been rewritten.

From across the terminal, I would have looked unremarkable.

Just another man in a dark jacket, headphones on, bag rolling behind him. Hands in his pockets. Stepping off the escalator with the kind of ease that suggests this has never been hard.

But I knew. I knew what that moment meant. I knew what it represented. I knew what it confirmed. *Soft Eyes, Strong Spine* is more than a posture. It's a nervous system reality. You can't fake it. You can't force it. You can't white-knuckle your way into calm.

Calm either lives in you … or it doesn't. And now finally it lived in me.

FIELD NOTES
What Strong Spine Feels Like in the Body

Shoulders sit lower without correction.

Breath lands deeper and stays there.

Thoughts don't outrun the moment.

Internal muscles aren't bracing for impact.

Ordinary tasks feel truly ordinary.

Time doesn't compress under pressure.

The world loses its sharp edges.

This is not relaxation. This is integration.

The Hidden Lesson of the Escalator

The real magic wasn't that I rode the escalator calmly. It's that nothing inside me was pretending. No self-talk. No tricks. No coping strategies. No mental negotiations. Just being carried upward without needing control by a structure I finally trusted.

That's the secret truth of transformation. The old fears don't vanish. They simply stop owning you. And once the body understands the new code, the world that used to scare you becomes just scenery again. Here's the truth no one tells you about becoming a different man: There's no ribbon-cutting. No ceremony. No chapter break in your life that announces, "Congratulations, you've arrived."

What actually happens is quieter. You move through your day—the Detroit airport, car rides, gym mornings, work decisions, small exchanges with your kids—and the world that once felt sharp or loud or demanding now feels spacious.

You respond without rushing.
You choose without fear.
You breathe without stiffening.
You listen without absorbing.

And slowly, almost imperceptibly, the world stops feeling like something that might collapse under you. Instead, you begin to feel something unfamiliar. Readiness.

A Strong Spine is not a finish line. It's a posture that prepares you for the future without dragging the past behind you. And that's what I felt walking across the terminal that day. Not triumph, not relief, not even pride. Just readiness. A sense that I could now move into the next act of my life with strength, with a new masculine.

Life Without the Old Internal Static

For most of my life, even in good seasons, there was always

static in the background, the hum of "what if," the buzz of "don't screw this up," the mental math of responsibility, the worry that one misstep could bring everything down, the belief that emotional vigilance was the price of being a good man.

But 2.0 revealed something radical. When a man stops hardening, the world doesn't fall apart. He stops falling apart inside it. There were days when I would sit in a hotel room at night and truly feel nothing in the best possible way—no dread, no tension, no scanning. It wasn't numbness. It was the absence of fear.

This is the space Chapter 17 will rise from. Not the collapse of the man I was, but the freeing of the man I became. *A Man Who Can Finally Walk Forward.* Life is forward-facing. Always has been.

A Strong Spine does one essential thing. It aligns the man with his own direction. When your nervous system isn't looking over its shoulder, your life stops being about survival and starts being about expansion.

Your kids feel it first. Your work feels it next. Your friendships recalibrate around it. Your decisions get cleaner. Your boundaries get quieter. Your body stops sending danger signals that were never necessary.

And the world becomes navigable again, not because it changed, but because your posture toward it did. This is where I found myself as the escalator delivered me into the upper terminal. Standing in the middle of Detroit Metro Airport, gate announcements bouncing off the high ceilings, the smell of coffee and pretzel-salt tucked into the air, with nothing flinching inside me, and the clean, unmistakable sense that the rest of my life was finally open.

Not easy. Not predictable. Not mapped. Just open.

The Ultra-Subtle Fatherline Echo

Here's where Tom comes in lightly, subtly, correctly for this chapter. There was a moment so small I almost missed it as I stepped off that escalator and began walking toward security.

A memory didn't appear. A voice didn't speak. A montage didn't roll. It was something quieter, a familiar steadiness in the way I moved. Not his jokes. Not his swagger. Not his cadence. Just the feeling I used to have when I walked beside him as a kid. That subtle, unspoken confidence he carried, that sense that he wasn't coiling against his own life.

It wasn't nostalgia. It wasn't grief. It wasn't even longing. It was a physiological echo, the lineage of calm passing forward in the man I had become without ever trying to imitate him.

This is how fathers stay alive in their sons—not through memory but through posture. A strong spine doesn't erase where you came from. It honors it by evolving it.

The Quiet Future Taking Shape

When a man stops tensing, the future stops feeling like something to survive. It becomes something to build. Not fast. Not dramatically. Not with frantic energy. But steadily. Brick by brick. Choice by choice. Day by day.

The future now feels spacious in a way it never did before. Not because life got easier; it didn't. But because I'm no longer fighting old battles in new rooms. There's nothing pulling me backward. No magnetic fear. No invisible tightness. No inherited script telling me danger lives in the next turn.

What I feel instead is momentum. Not the strained kind, but

the natural, gravity-assisted kind that arrives when a man stops placing his own foot on the brake. At Paul's funeral, the thought had come quietly and stayed. My big three—Paul, Tom, and Mark —were all gone. Now I didn't try to make meaning out of it or turn it into a moment. It was just a clean fact, landing where facts land.

For most of my life, my steadiness lived outside of me. I leaned on certain men as reference points—how they carried themselves, how they stayed grounded without needing to explain it. I didn't know I was doing that at the time. I just was.

Standing here now, I can feel what changed. Not suddenly. Not loudly. Just steadily. They're still part of me, but I'm not waiting on them anymore. The weight rests somewhere different now.

This is the emotional on-ramp to the final chapter. This is the state a man must reach before he can step into Part V's true promise. The Return. The Wide Open Road. The Life Lived Forward.

Every story with a real transformation has a moment like this, a moment where the reader can feel the character gathering himself, not for conflict but for continuation. That's what this chapter is. Not the climax. Not the peak. Not the ending. The breath before the horizon. The inhalation before the stride.

The moment where the man finally aligned with himself is ready to walk out of the airport, into his life, and into the chapter that will carry the full emotional weight of the book's close. The Wide Open Road. This is the part where you can feel the road opening up.

Not because life turns easy. Because you stop making everything heavier than it needs to be. You stop negotiating with the noise. You stop living like the next corner is where danger lives.

It doesn't feel like fireworks. It feels like forward motion. Like easing off the brake. Like you can look forward without that old tightness in your chest trying to run the whole show.

If you've made it this far, you already know the difference: Tightening is loud. Steadiness is quiet. And quiet is where your real strength has been hiding.

NOTES FROM A DIVORCED DAD
What to Carry Forward

- Boundaries protect warmth, they don't cancel it
- Calm is portable; it travels into hard rooms
- Integrity isn't loud, it's consistent
- You can hold your line without escalating the moment
- Strong Spine is how you stay you

CHAPTER 17

LIVING FORWARD

Living the Rest of Your Life Awake

By the time you reach this page, the bridges are still there. So are the escalators, the long pauses, the meetings that used to throw your system off balance. The world hasn't settled down. You have.

You still fly out of CLT. You still walk the jetway. You still hear the safety spiel and the soft ding of the seatbelt sign. But inside, something is different.

You're not the son watching his father fall. You're not the man pacing a loud house, trying to hold it all up. You're not behind the wheel, talking past an apology. You're not staring at a name on your phone, hoping this time the words land.

You're just here. A man at a gate. Heart beating. Spine steady. Breath low and slow. Carry-on tucked beneath your feet. The low hum of other people's lives folding into the rhythm of your own. And that's enough.

Today I'm at Gate B6. It's the same terminal I've crossed for years. The air carries that familiar airport mix—hand sanitizer and recycled air. Overhead announcements blur into one another, just fragments of city names and boarding groups.

The PA chime cuts through every few minutes, and the wheels of rolling bags make that soft rattle that sounds like everybody moving on at once. A kid a few seats down leans against his mother's shoulder. His hoodie is bunched like a pillow; her hand rests on his hair without thinking about it.

A couple scrolls in silence. A pilot walks by with a coffee, eyes somewhere between home and wherever he's headed next. Nothing dramatic is happening. That's the point. There were years when a moment like this felt unbearable. Too quiet, too unstructured, too much room for my nervous system to invent disaster.

Three seats over, a man in work boots stares at the departure board like it owes him money. His hands are big, cracked at the knuckles. Wedding ring? No ring. Doesn't matter. He's doing the same thing I used to do—trying to act like he isn't carrying a whole life in his chest.

Across from him, another guy about my age sips a drink and keeps checking his phone, like the next vibration is going to tell him he didn't miss it. Not the flight. The moment. The kid. The marriage. The version of himself that used to laugh easily.

That's the quiet thing you start to notice when you stop locking up. There are men everywhere holding their breath. Some of them don't even know it.

For years, I would sit in a chair like this and feel my chest tighten, my brain sprinting ahead to flights, connections, kids, work, money, marriage, divorce—whatever problem I could drag into the present.

Now Gate B6 feels different. Same concourse. Same airline. Same early-morning light. New frequency. This is what the open road actually feels like in a man's body. Not adrenaline, not reinvention, not some cinematic reset, but a quiet permission to exist inside your own life. To sit in a plastic airport chair and not be at war with any of it.

I catch my reflection in the dark glass of the window—not a dramatic moment, just a quick glimpse. Same face. Same lines. But the eyes are different. Softer. Like I'm not scanning for trouble.

My phone buzzes. I don't lunge for it. I glance, decide, and slide it back into my pocket. Even that is a dial now—not on or off, not panicked or numb. Just choice. Volume where I set it.

FIELD NOTES
Reflection: Your Own Open Road

Take five quiet minutes and ask yourself:
Where am I still gripping?
What small moment this week could I let be
enough?
If the people I love could describe my energy in
one word, what do I hope it is?

Not perfect. Not impressive.
Something like—Steady. Calm. Solid. Kind.

That's the work.
One breath at a time. One boundary at a time.

One unsent text at a time.

Pick one. Do it once. That counts.

A Turn Toward Home

Airports teach you about open space. But the real test of a man's new frequency happens in the rooms where his kids live their real lives. The open road isn't out there. It's in the places where the old version of you once tightened, and the new version of you stays steady.

Not long after Detroit, I found myself sitting in a high school auditorium one county over—stage lights, heavy curtains, the familiar smell of varnished wood and winter coats.

It was a Sunday afternoon. Connor was playing with the area community band, a local mix of grown-ups and kids and retired guys who still remember what it feels like to be part of something that asks for discipline and gives back music.

I drove there alone. He was picking up a friend, so he drove out there in his car. The parking lot was full in that soft Sunday way. No rush-hour edge. Just families walking in small clusters, hands in pockets, shoulders hunched against a cool early winter day.

Inside, it was a typical high school auditorium—rows of seats, a stage. But this one had more light than most. The kind of natural light that sneaks in from the sides and makes the whole room feel less like a cave.

I took a seat about halfway back. Not hiding. Not performing. Just sitting. A folded program rested in my hands—glossy paper, the song list printed in that standard concert font that looks the same in every town.

I came in without scanning the crowd. I didn't need to know who was there to make it real. I just wanted to watch my son play.

During a break between songs, I turned my head to the right and there she was—Connor's mother. Sitting quiet, composed. Just a face in the crowd, but not just any face. We've shared rooms like this before—school plays, courtrooms, birthdays, paperwork. I took her in for a beat. Familiar terrain. Old muscle memory. Then I turned back toward the stage.

In the old days, seeing the ex-wife like this—across a room, no words exchanged—changed my breathing. Not because anything bad was happening. Just because my wiring assumed it might. My posture would tense. My pulse would start taking notes. The internal weather system would spin up.

My body did what it's done for years—that quiet stiffening, the subtle armor sliding into place, like I was preparing for a hit I couldn't see coming.

Then I caught it. The tension was mine. Not something she was doing—something I was doing. Bracing for an impact that never came.

And the truth landed, plain as day: She never made a scene in public. Whatever wars we had, they were behind closed doors, like most divorced couples. In a room full of strangers, we always held it together.

That meant the danger I'd been preparing for in places like this—the imagined explosion, the public humiliation, the sideways comment loud enough for other people to hear—was mostly a movie my nervous system kept replaying.

So I didn't turn toward her. I didn't avoid her. I didn't make eye contact. I didn't send a signal. I just let her be a person in a seat and let myself be a man in mine.

That's what 2.0 looks like sometimes: Stepping back far enough to allow you to name the pattern without becoming it. Keeping that emotional baggage parked someplace else. But now? The air stays calm. The fluorescent lights hum overhead, steady, indifferent.

Onstage, the community band is assembled in black concert attire. A few whisper last-second instructions. A percussion kid drops a stick, blushes, retrieves it. Life continues. The room carries that faint metallic warmth of bodies breathing, radiators working, a little perfume, and somehow a trace of popcorn, like it's game day even though it isn't.

Then I see him. Connor sits in the middle of the arrangement, tenor sax in hand. Same black outfit. Same deliberate pace. And my body registers him instantly the way only a parent's body can.

He adjusts his music stand, shifts his weight, wipes his palms on his pants in a gesture that is pure seventeen-year-old humanity. The sax strap sits right. The reed is just so.

He looks older than yesterday and younger than next year, both true at once. I don't tighten. I don't narrate. I don't future-cast. I just watch my son exist in his own life.

The conductor raises her hands. The room settles into silence. The first note blooms—uncertain, then confident—and the music gathers the gym into something whole. Christmas songs, familiar and clean. I stay where I am, breathing, present for the sound, for the boy on the stage, for the life that no longer requires me to lean forward.

Parents shift. Someone coughs. A sneaker squeaks somewhere down low. A phone screen flashes and goes dark again. The auditorium continues being an auditorium.

Then they announce a piece where a small group steps out—five woodwinds together for a short passage—and I watch Connor move into position with that careful confidence you only get from weekly rehearsals and a couple concerts a year that make the practice real.

During the smallest pocket of stillness, he lifts his head. His eyes move across the room, searching for something steady. And he finds me. For half a second, nothing in the world is trying to be anything else.

He makes eye contact, gives me a half smile, then it's gone, just a quiet checkin that says, I know you're there. No performance. No message. Just a clean signal.

It settles in my chest with a gentle weight—not as a payoff or a repair, but as something rarer: a moment my nervous system is finally steady enough to receive without trying to hold it.

Around us, the music swells again. Connor looks away and reorients himself to the notes. And I sit there steady, breathing slow, letting the moment be exactly what it is.

The Wide Open Road isn't a highway. It's an auditorium chair, a winter concert, an ex-wife nearby, a son onstage, and the unshakable feeling that nothing in this room needs to be controlled for me to feel at home in my own life.

The fog has cleared. I'm the one at the wheel now. The song ends. Applause rises. Connor resets his hands and continues. I remain in my seat—steady, present, grounded. Nothing more. Nothing less. Just enough.

The show ended. The applause came and went. The chairs scraped. People stood and stretched like they'd been holding their own breath the whole time. Connor had to finish up, so we would meet at home.

I didn't look for my ex after the show. I didn't avoid her either. I just walked out when it was time, the same way I walked in—alone, steady, not looking for contact and not afraid of it.

In the parking lot, that old reflex tried one last time. Tighten. Scan. Prepare. I noticed it the way you notice a song you once used to play on repeat. Familiar. Not in charge. I got in my car and turned the heat up one notch. Another dial. Another choice.

At home, I set the concert program on the counter without thinking. It sat there like a small receipt from a life I'm still building.

Later that night Connor walked in and saw it. I've saved every one of his programs since high school started, and he knows it, not because I announce it, but because the stack exists.

He picked it up, glanced at the songs, and we talked about the show for a minute. Nothing deep. Just warm. Just honest connection. A quick exchange that said: "I saw you. I was there."

Then he went to his room. I looked at the program on the counter and felt it—no spike, no scramble. Just open space.

It was elegant and beautiful, my own movie ending in a simple way. A man who isn't running his life from fear anymore.

NOTES FROM A DIVORCED DAD
What to Carry Forward

- You don't need a breakthrough to move forward, you need steadiness you can repeat

- Most moments don't ask for fixing, they ask for you not to flinch
- If you feel space where there used to be panic, don't fill it—that's the upgrade
- Fear doesn't disappear when life gets easier—it disappears when you stop letting it drive

Dying isn't scary
Living scared is

EPILOGUE

By the time you reach the end of this book, your life may look much the same on the surface. The calendar fills. The past carries its memory. People arrive with their own weather.

What's different is you.

Something inside you has settled. You recognize your own signals more quickly. You notice when your shoulders rise, when your breath shortens, when an old name enters the room. And you know what you're feeling.

You can tell the difference between a real threat and an old habit. You can stay in your seat—steady, present, grounded—even as the moment moves around you.

Soft Eyes, Strong Spine together lets you move forward steady enough to love. Clear enough to lead. Calm enough to stay yourself when things get loud.

This isn't the end of the work. It's the posture you carry into the rest of your life. There may be days you forget. Days you go quiet in the old way and call it "fine." That doesn't mean you lost anything. It means you're human.

The win isn't perfection. The win is coming back faster—

without punishing yourself, without blaming anyone else, without needing a dramatic reset.

If this book helped you breathe a little easier, you're not alone. It was written by a man who had to learn the same lessons the hard way—slowly and imperfectly. Much of it was written in ordinary places—airport gates, quiet parking lots, late-night kitchens—because that's where this kind of change actually shows up.

Carry what's useful. Leave the rest. And if you ever catch yourself tightening again, remember: Awareness is already release.

ACKNOWLEDGMENTS

This book was shaped by the men I watched closely. The ones who stayed when things were uncomfortable, who listened without fixing, who told the truth cleanly and didn't flinch—thank you. You showed me what steadiness looks like long before I had language for it, long before I knew what that kind of presence feels like to receive.

To the women who showed me what it feels like to be met by a man who is actually there. You changed how I understand presence. Even when things didn't last, the lessons did.

To those who read early drafts and said, "Keep going," before the voice had fully settled. Your patience mattered.

And to anyone holding this book and trying to live a little less scared than they used to: I see you. Thank you for reading.

ABOUT THE AUTHOR

Eric Brockman is a father of four and a longtime sales professional in the aerospace composites industry. Much of his learning happened outside of work—in airports, gyms, kitchens, and quiet drives with his sons. After his second divorce, he began paying attention to what actually steadied a room and what didn't. Over time, his focus narrowed to the things that held.

Eric writes about a form of masculinity that doesn't rely on force or performance but on steadiness, emotional clarity, and the ability to stay present when things get loud. *Soft Eyes, Strong Spine* is his first book.

Eric lives in North Carolina, where he fishes, watches sports, writes in the mornings, and continues practicing the simple code that changed his life.

www.ingramcontent.com/pod-product-compliance
Lightning Source LLC
Chambersburg PA
CBHW061423150726
47987CB00001B/68